Tolley's Capital Gain
2021–22

by

Kevin Walton MA

Tolley®

Tolley's Capital Gains Tax 2021–22

LexisNexis® UK & Worldwide

United Kingdom	RELX (UK) Limited trading as LexisNexis®, 1–3 Strand, London WC2N 5JR and 9–10 St Andrew Square, Edinburgh EH2 2AF
LNUK Global Partners	LexisNexis® encompasses authoritative legal publishing brands dating back to the 19th century including: Butterworths® in the United Kingdom, Canada and the Asia-Pacific region; Les Editions du Juris Classeur in France; and Matthew Bender® worldwide. Details of LexisNexis® locations worldwide can be found at www.lexisnexis.com

© 2021 RELX (UK) Ltd.

Published by LexisNexis®
This is a Tolley title

All rights reserved. No part of this publication may be reproduced in any material form (including photocopying or storing it in any medium by electronic means and whether or not transiently or incidentally to some other use of this publication) without the written permission of the copyright owner except in accordance with the provisions of the Copyright, Designs and Patents Act 1988 or under the terms of a licence issued by the Copyright Licensing Agency Ltd, Saffron House, 6–10 Kirby Street, London EC1N 8TS. Applications for the copyright owner's written permission to reproduce any part of this publication should be addressed to the publisher.
Warning: The doing of an unauthorised act in relation to a copyright work may result in both a civil claim for damages and criminal prosecution.

Crown copyright material is reproduced with the permission of the Controller of HMSO and the Queen's Printer for Scotland. Parliamentary copyright material is reproduced with the permission of the Controller of Her Majesty's Stationery Office on behalf of Parliament. Any European material in this work which has been reproduced from EUR-lex, the official European Communities legislation website, is European Communities copyright.

LexisNexis® and the Knowledge Burst logo are registered trademarks of RELX Group plc, used under license. Butterworths® and Tolley® are registered trademarks of RELX (UK) Ltd. Matthew Bender® is a registered trademark of Matthew Bender & Company Inc. Other products and services may be trademarks or registered trademarks of their respective companies.
A CIP Catalogue record for this book is available from the British Library.

ISBN for this volume: 9780754557630

Printed and bound by CPI Group (UK) Ltd, Croydon, CR0 4YY

Visit LexisNexis UK at www.lexisnexis.co.uk

About This Book

The text of this work includes full coverage of Finance Act 2021 and all other relevant material to 1 July 2021 e.g. statutes, statutory instruments, court cases, Tribunal decisions, press releases, concessions, Statements of Practice, HMRC Briefs, and other publications.

We welcome all comments and suggestions for improvement to this work. You can contact us in this respect by e-mailing the Editor, Gemma Murray at Gemma.Murray@lexisnexis.co.uk. Any technical queries will be passed on to the author.

Tolley's Capital Gains Tax 2021/22 sets out the position for 2021/22 and the four preceding years, i.e. for 2017/18 to 2020/21, but some references are still required to earlier years.

The approach which has been adopted to statutory references in this work is as follows.

(i) References to current legislation invariably quote the *TCGA 1992* reference in the familiar form, i.e. '*TCGA 1992, s XXX*' to identify a section and '*TCGA 1992, Sch XX*' to identify a Schedule. Where there has been no change in the legislation in the last four years, no statutory reference other than the current legislation is quoted.

(ii) Where the legislation has changed during the last four years, the earlier provisions continue to be described in the text, and the appropriate earlier statutory reference is quoted. Legislation current during those four years but now repealed is similarly dealt with. Where any part of the current legislation was introduced during those four years, the commencement date is quoted.

Contents

About This Book		v
Abbreviations and References		xi
1	Introduction to capital gains tax	
2	Annual Rates and Exemptions	
3	Alternative Finance Arrangements	
4	Anti-Avoidance	
5	Appeals	
6	Assessments	
7	Assets	
8	Assets held on 6 April 1965	
9	Assets held on 31 March 1982	
10	Business Asset Disposal Relief (formerly Entrepreneurs' Relief)	
11	Capital Sums Derived from Assets	
12	Charities	
13	Children	
14	Claims	
15	Companies	
16	Companies — Corporate Finance and Intangibles	
17	Computation of Gains and Losses	
18	Connected Persons	
19	Corporate Venturing Scheme	
20	Death	
21	Disclosure of Tax Avoidance Schemes	
22	Double Tax Relief	
23	Employee Share Schemes	
24	Enterprise Investment Scheme	
25	Exemptions and Reliefs	
26	Furnished Holiday Accommodation	
27	Gifts	
28	Government Securities	
29	Groups of Companies	
30	HMRC — Administration	

Contents

31	HMRC — Confidentiality of Information
32	HMRC Explanatory Publications
33	HMRC Extra-Statutory Concessions
34	HMRC Investigatory Powers
35	HMRC Statements of Practice
36	Hold-Over Reliefs
37	Incorporation and Disincorporation Reliefs
38	Indexation
39	Interaction with Other Taxes
40	Investors' Relief
41	Land
42	Late Payment Interest and Penalties
43	Life Insurance Policies and Deferred Annuities
44	Losses
45	Market Value
46	Married Persons and Civil Partners
47	Mineral Royalties
48	Offshore Settlements
49	Overseas Matters
50	Partnerships
51	Payment of Tax
52	Penalties
53	Private Residences
54	Qualifying Corporate Bonds
55	Remittance Basis
56	Repayment Interest
57	Residence and Domicile
58	Returns
59	Rollover Relief — Replacement of Business Assets
60	Seed Enterprise Investment Scheme
61	Self-Assessment
62	Settlements
63	Shares and Securities
64	Shares and Securities — Identification Rules
65	Social Investment Relief
66	Substantial Shareholding Exemption
67	Time Limits — Fixed Dates

68	**Time Limits — Miscellaneous**
69	**Underwriters at Lloyd's**
70	**Unit Trusts and Other Investment Vehicles**
71	**Venture Capital Trusts**
72	**Wasting Assets**
73	**Finance Act 2021 — Summary of CGT Provisions**
74	**Tax Case Digest**
75	**Table of Statutes**
76	**Table of Statutory Instruments**
77	**Table of Cases**
78	**Index**

Abbreviations and References

Abbreviations

A-G	Attorney-General.
Art	Article.
BES	Business Expansion Scheme.
CA	Court of Appeal.
CAA	Capital Allowances Act.
CCA	Court of Criminal Appeal.
CCAB	Consultative Committee of Accountancy Bodies.
CES	Court of Exchequer (Scotland).
Cf.	compare.
CGT	Capital Gains Tax.
CGTA	Capital Gains Tax Act.
CJEC	Court of Justice of the European Communities.
Ch D	Chancery Division.
CIR	Commissioners of Inland Revenue ('the Board' or 'the Revenue').
CRCA	Commissioners for Revenue and Customs Act.
CTA	Corporation Tax Act.
DC	Divisional Court.
EC	European Community.
ECHR	European Court of Human Rights.
EIS	Enterprise Investment Scheme.
ESC	HMRC Extra-Statutory Concession.
EU	European Union.
Ex D	Exchequer Division (now part of Chancery Division).
FA	Finance Act.
Fam D	Family Division.

FTT	First-tier Tribunal.
HC	House of Commons.
HL	House of Lords.
HMRC	Her Majesty's Revenue and Customs.
I	Ireland.
ICAEW	Institute of Chartered Accountants in England and Wales.
ICTA	Income and Corporation Taxes Act.
IHT	Inheritance Tax.
IHTA	Inheritance Tax Act.
ISA	Individual Savings Account.
ITA	Income Tax Act.
ITEPA	Income Tax (Earnings and Pensions) Act.
ITTOIA	Income Tax (Trading and Other Income) Act.
KB	King's Bench Division.
LLP	Limited Liability Partnership.
LLPA	Limited Liability Partnership Act.
NI	Northern Ireland.
OEIC	Open-ended Investment Company
PC	Privy Council.
PDA	Probate, Divorce and Admiralty Division (now Family Division).
PEP	Personal Equity Plan.
QB	Queen's Bench Division.
QIS	Qualified Investor Scheme
R	Regina or Rex (i.e. The Crown).
Reg	Regulation.
RPI	Retail Prices Index.
s	Section.
SC	Supreme Court.
SC(I)	Supreme Court (Ireland).
SCS	Scottish Court of Session.
Sch	Schedule.
SE	*Societas Europaea* (European Company)

Abbreviations and References

SI	Statutory Instrument.
SP	HMRC Statement of Practice.
Sp C	Special Commissioners.
TCEA	Tribunals, Courts and Enforcement Act.
TCGA	Taxation of Chargeable Gains Act.
TIOPA	Taxation (International and Other Provisions) Act.
TMA	Taxes Management Act.
UT	Upper Tribunal.

References

(*denotes a series accredited for citation in court).

All ER	*All England Law Reports (LexisNexis).
All ER(D)	All England Reporter Direct (LexisNexis).
AC	*Law Reports, Appeal Cases (Incorporated Council of Law Reporting for England and Wales).
ATC	*Annotated Tax Cases (publication discontinued).
Ch	*Law Reports, Chancery Division.
CMLR	Common Market Law Reports.
Ex D	Law Reports, Exchequer Division (1875–1880; see also below).
Fam D	*Law Reports, Family Division.
KB	*Law Reports, King's Bench Division (1900–1952).
IR	*Irish Reports (Incorporated Council of Law Reporting for Ireland).
ITC	*Irish Tax Cases.
LR Ex	*Law Reports, Exchequer Division (1865–1875; see also above).
NILR	Northern Ireland Law Reports.
QB	*Law Reports, Queen's Bench Division (1891–1901 and 1952 onwards).
QBD	Law Reports, Queen's Bench Division (1875–1890).
SFTD	*Simon's First-tier Tax Decisions (LexisNexis).

SLT	Scots Law Times.
Sp C	Special Commissioner's Decisions.
SSCD	Simon's Tax Cases—Special Commissioners' Decisions (LexisNexis).
STC	*Simon's Tax Cases (LexisNexis).
SWTI	Simon's Weekly Tax Intelligence (LexisNexis).
TC	*Official Reports of Tax Cases.
TR	Taxation Reports (publication discontinued).
WLR	*Weekly Law Reports (Incorporated Council of Law Reporting).

The first number in the citation refers to the volume, and the second to the page, so that [1978] 2 WLR 10 means that the report is to be found on page ten of the second volume of the Weekly Law Reports for 1978. Where no volume number is given, only one volume was produced in that year. Some series have continuous volume numbers.

Where legal decisions are very recent and in the lower courts, it must be remembered that they may be reversed on appeal. However, references to the official Tax Cases ('TC'), and to the Appeal Cases ('AC') may be taken as final.

In English cases, Scottish and Northern Irish decisions (unless there is a difference of law between the countries) are generally followed but are not binding, and Republic of Ireland decisions are considered (and vice versa).

1

Introduction to capital gains tax

Basic principles of capital gains tax	1.1
The charge to tax	1.2
Brexit	1.3
Coronavirus (COVID-19)	1.4
Key points on the charge to capital gains tax	1.5

Basic principles of capital gains tax

[1.1] Capital gains tax is charged on chargeable gains made by individuals, personal representatives and trustees on the disposal of ASSETS (7.2). The tax is chargeable on the total gains on disposals in a 'tax year', after deductions, including LOSSES (44) and the annual exempt amount (see 2 ANNUAL RATES AND EXEMPTIONS). Every gain is a chargeable gain unless expressly excluded (see 25 EXEMPTIONS AND RELIEFS). For this purpose, a *'tax year'*, otherwise known as a *'year of assessment'*, is a year ending on 5 April. Thus '2021/22' indicates the tax year ending on 5 April 2022 (and so on). [*TCGA 1992, s 288(1)(1ZA)*].

Companies and other corporate bodies within the scope of corporation tax do not pay capital gains tax as such but instead are chargeable to corporation tax on their chargeable gains. The computation of their gains is now significantly different from the computation principles applying for capital gains tax (see **15.2** COMPANIES). Companies pay corporation tax by reference to accounting periods rather than years of assessment.

For both capital gains tax and corporation tax purposes, a gain is computed by reference to the excess of the disposal consideration over the acquisition consideration, received and given, for an asset. In certain circumstances the legislation deems a disposal or acquisition to take place where there is no actual disposal or acquisition. Certain types of expenditure are deductible in computing the gain. See **17** COMPUTATION OF GAINS AND LOSSES. Companies are given an allowance, known as the indexation allowance (see **38** INDEXATION), which for each gain adjusts for the effects of inflation. Indexation allowance has now been frozen at its December 2017 level. For CGT purposes, gains on certain business disposals may, subject to a lifetime limit, qualify for BUSINESS ASSET DISPOSAL RELIEF (**10**) (formerly known as entrepreneurs' relief). Similarly, gains on certain disposals after 5 April 2019 by individuals of shares in unlisted trading companies may, subject to a lifetime limit, qualify for INVESTORS' RELIEF (**40**). Business asset disposal relief and investors' relief do not apply for the purposes of corporation tax on chargeable gains.

Capital gains tax (CGT) was introduced by *FA 1965* and commenced on 6 April 1965. The legislation was consolidated by *CGTA 1979* and subsequently by *TCGA 1992*. Assets acquired before 7 April 1965 are within the charge if they

[1.1] Introduction to capital gains tax

are disposed of on or after that date, but there are special provisions dealing with the computation of gains on the disposal of such assets (see 8 ASSETS HELD ON 6 APRIL 1965). *FA 1988* replaced the 1965 base date with 31 March 1982, subject to the detailed provisions of ASSETS HELD ON 31 MARCH 1982 (9). For CGT purposes, re-basing to 31 March 1982 applies to all assets held on that date without exception. Exceptions continue to apply for corporation tax purposes.

Both CGT and corporation tax are administered and paid under SELF-ASSESSMENT (61). For disposals on or after 6 April 2020, a special compliance regime applies to all direct disposals of UK land where a residential property gain arises. A UK land disposal return must be made together with a payment on account of CGT on or before the 30th day following the day of the completion of the disposal. See 51.3 PAYMENT OF TAX and 58.21 RETURNS. Previously, the regime applied only to non-UK residents (see 58.21, 58.22 RETURNS).

For individuals, gains are treated as if they were the top slice of the taxpayer's income. To the extent that gains fall within the basic rate band, they are taxable at 10% unless the gains are on disposals of residential property or carried interest, in which case, they are taxable at 18%. Where they exceed the basic rate band limit, gains are taxable at 20% or, for gains on disposals of residential property or carried interest, 28%. Trustees of settlements and personal representatives are chargeable to CGT at 20% or, for gains on disposals of residential property or carried interest, 28%. See 2 ANNUAL RATES AND EXEMPTIONS. For companies, chargeable gains form part of the taxable total profits and are accordingly taxable at the appropriate corporation tax rate. See 15 COMPANIES.

The charge to tax

[1.2] Subject to exceptions and special provisions, a person is chargeable to capital gains tax in respect of chargeable gains accruing to them in a tax year if they are resident in the UK during any part of the tax year. The charge applies to gains on assets situated both in the UK and overseas. In the case of personal representatives of a deceased person, the person in question is the deemed single and continuing body in 20.9 DEATH. In the case of the trustees of a settlement, the person in question is the deemed single person in 48.1 OFFSHORE SETTLEMENTS.

A person who is not resident in the UK during any part of a tax year is also chargeable to capital gains tax but only in respect of chargeable gains accruing in that year on the disposal of:

(i) UK-situated assets with a connection to the person's UK branch or agency (see 49.3 OVERSEAS MATTERS);
(ii) (for disposals on or after 6 April 2019) interests in UK land (see 41.23 LAND) or (for disposals before that date but on or after 6 April 2015) interests in UK residential property (see 41.31 LAND); and
(iii) (for disposals on or after 6 April 2019) assets deriving at least 75% of their value from UK land where the person has a substantial indirect interest in that land (see 41.24 LAND).

If the tax year is a split year for an individual under the statutory residence test (see **57.17** RESIDENCE AND DOMICILE), gains accruing in the overseas part of the year are only chargeable to capital gains tax if the assets disposed of are within (i)–(iii) above. This rule is subject to the charge on temporary non-residents (see **49.5** OVERSEAS MATTERS).

[*TCGA 1992, ss 1(1), 1A, 1G(2); FA 2019, Sch 1 paras 2, 120*].

Note that for 2018/19 and earlier years, these provisions were contained in *TCGA 1992, ss 1(1), 2(1)–(1C), 14B, 14D(1)* (as originally enacted).

Companies are not chargeable to capital gains tax, but instead are chargeable to corporation tax in respect of their chargeable gains. [*TCGA 1992, s 1(2); FA 2019, Sch 1 para 2*]. UK-resident companies are chargeable to corporation tax on gains on assets situated in the UK or overseas. Non-resident companies are chargeable to corporation tax only on chargeable gains on the disposal of:

(a) UK-situated assets with a connection to the company's UK permanent establishment (see **49.3** OVERSEAS MATTERS);
(b) (for disposals on or after 6 April 2019) interests in UK land (see **41.23** LAND); and
(c) (for disposals on or after 6 April 2019) assets deriving at least 75% of their value from UK land where the company has a substantial indirect interest in that land (see **41.24** LAND).

For disposals before 6 April 2019, there were two exceptions to the rule that companies are not chargeable to capital gains tax. The exceptions were for the capital gains tax charges on high value disposals of dwellings (see **15.12** COMPANIES) and non-resident disposals of UK residential property interests (see **41.31** LAND). For later disposals the charge on high value disposals of dwellings is abolished and the charge on UK residential property interests is replaced by the corporation tax charge in (b) above.

[*TCGA 1992, s 2; FA 2019, Sch 1 paras 2, 120*].

See **15** COMPANIES and **57.32** RESIDENCE AND DOMICILE.

Special rules apply to persons not resident or individuals not domiciled in the UK, to temporary visitors to the UK and to persons becoming temporarily non-UK resident. See **49** OVERSEAS MATTERS, **50** PARTNERSHIPS, **56** REPAYMENT INTEREST and **57** RESIDENCE AND DOMICILE.

Married persons and civil partners are taxed independently. Transfers between spouses or civil partners living together are made on a 'no gain, no loss' basis. See **46** MARRIED PERSONS AND CIVIL PARTNERS.

Persons may be assessed in a representative capacity. See **6** ASSESSMENTS, **20** DEATH, **61** SELF-ASSESSMENT and **62** SETTLEMENTS.

There are special rules for UK resident shareholders of certain overseas resident companies. See **49.7** OVERSEAS MATTERS. See **48** OFFSHORE SETTLEMENTS for the provisions applying to trustees, settlors and beneficiaries of settlements which are or become overseas resident.

For unit and investment trusts, real estate investment trusts, open-ended investment companies and qualifying investor schemes, see **70** UNIT TRUSTS AND OTHER INVESTMENT VEHICLES. For venture capital trusts, see **71.10** VENTURE CAPITAL TRUSTS.

TCGA 1992, ss 194–198I, which deal with matters relating to oil exploration taxed under the *Oil Taxation Act 1975* and in practice apply mainly to companies, are not dealt with in this book.

Brexit

[1.3] The UK left the European Union on 31 January 2020. An 11-month implementation period (or 'transition period') applied up to 31 December 2020 during which the UK continued to be subject to current EU laws, remaining a member of the Single Market and Customs Union.

On 24 December 2020, the European Commission and UK Government announced an agreement in principle on the legal terms of the future EU-UK relationship – the (draft) EU-UK Trade and Cooperation Agreement (TCA). The TCA was signed by UK and EU leaders and then approved by the UK Parliament on 30 December 2020 and applied provisionally until full ratification by the European Parliament with effect from 1 May 2021. The UK has enacted the *EU (Future Relationship) Act 2020*, which makes provision to implement the TCA in the UK.

The majority of key domestic tax changes associated with Brexit take effect from the end of the implementation period (specifically, 11pm (GMT) on 31 December 2020, referred to as 'IP completion day'), including the full repeal of the *European Communities Act 1972*, incorporation of retained EU law (see below) into the UK domestic legal regime, and the commencement of associated Brexit legislation and statutory instruments.

Retained EU law is a collective term given to the body of EU-derived laws preserved and converted into domestic UK law at IP completion day when the repeal of the *European Communities Act 1972* took effect. As with other domestic law, it can be amended or repealed in the future. EU law that was not retained ceased to apply in relation to the UK following the end of the transition period. Retained EU law falls into three categories:

(1) EU-derived domestic legislation – ie UK legislation which was enacted to give effect to EU legislation – for example, the mergers legislation (*TCGA 1992, ss 140* onwards, see **49.11** OVERSEAS MATTERS) which was introduced to implement the Mergers Directive;
(2) direct EU legislation – ie English language versions of EU regulations, EU decisions and EU tertiary legislation; and
(3) other rights, powers etc – these can include rights arising under Directives, but only if they are of a kind recognised by the Court of Justice in a case decided before IP completion day, or by a UK court or tribunal in a case begun before IP completion day.

[*EUWA 2018, ss 2, 3, 4*].

Judgments of the CJEU made before IP completion day are binding on the First-tier Tribunal, the Upper Tribunal and the High Court, in relation to disputes about the validity, meaning or effect of retained EU law. There is an exception if the law has been modified since IP completion day and it would be inconsistent with the intention of the modifications for the court or tribunal to follow the EU judgment. The Supreme Court, and the UK's higher appeals courts including the Court of Appeal in England and Wales, the Court of Appeal in Northern Ireland, and the Inner House of the Court of Session (in Scotland), are not bound by any judgments of the CJEU, whether made before or after IP completion day. In deciding whether to depart from a pre-IP completion day EU judgment, these courts must apply the same test as the Supreme Court applies in deciding whether to depart from its own case law, namely, whether it appears right to do so. Judgments of the Court of Justice made after IP completion day are not binding on UK tribunals or courts, but they may 'have regard' to those judgments if they are relevant to the matter being litigated. [*EUWA 2018, s 6; SI 2020 No 1525*].

Coronavirus (COVID-19)

[1.4] The coronavirus pandemic has led to a large number of measures announced by the Government and HMRC, including financial support for businesses and employees as well as a number of administrative changes and relaxations. The following are the measures relevant to tax on capital gains.

Appeals

A number of temporary changes have been made to the provisions relating to appeals. The main changes are as follows:

- HMRC will allow an extra three months on top of the normal 30-day time limit for making an appeal against a decision dated February 2020 or later where the taxpayer has been affected by coronavirus.
- The First-tier Tribunal issued a general stay on all proceedings on 24 March 2020 for 28 days until 21 April 2020.
- Appeals received by the First-tier Tribunal before 24 March 2020 and categorised as standard or complex before 21 April 2020 were subject to a further stay on proceedings until 30 June 2020.
- The existing limit of £2,000 for allocation by the First-tier Tribunal of penalty appeals to the default paper category is temporarily increased to £20,000. The increase was initially for six months but it has been extended until 30 June 2021.
- With effect from 10 April 2020, if a party objects to an appeal being decided on the papers, the First-tier Tribunal or Upper Tribunal may nevertheless decide that it should be decided in that way. However, the Tribunal can only take that step if the matter is urgent, it is not reasonably practicable for there to be a hearing (including one conducted wholly or partly by telephone or by video) and it is in the interests of justice to make that direction. This rule is expressed to expire at the same time as the *Coronavirus Act 2020*, i.e. on 24 March 2022 unless that date is either brought forward or extended.
- Hearings will be heard remotely (by telephone or video) where it is reasonably practicable and in accordance with the overriding objective to do so until 18 September 2021. A tribunal may decide to conduct a 'hybrid' hearing, where some participants are in a physical hearing room and others are attending remotely.

[1.4] Introduction to capital gains tax

- With effect from 10 April 2020, the First-tier Tribunal or Upper Tribunal may direct that a telephone or video hearing be heard in private if it is not possible for a media representative to listen to or watch the hearing at the time it is taking place and it is in the interests of justice for the hearing to be in private. If a hearing is held in private under this rule, it must be recorded. A hearing must also be recorded if it is public only by virtue of a media representative being able to access the proceedings remotely while they are taking place. These provisions expire at the same time as the *Coronavirus Act 2020*, i.e. on 24 March 2022, unless that date is either brought forward or extended.
- If a party fails to attend a telephone or video hearing without making an application for it to be adjourned, wins the appeal and then applies for the decision to be set aside on the basis of non-attendance, the Tribunal is unlikely to allow that application.

See **5.1** APPEALS.

Enterprise Investment Scheme and Seed Enterprise Investment Scheme

If an individual to whom shares in a company have been issued enters into a convertible loan agreement with the company under the Future Fund on or after 20 May 2020, and subsequently receives value from the company under the terms of that agreement, the value received is ignored for the purposes of EIS and SEIS income tax relief and EIS capital gains deferral relief. This is to ensure that investors in a company who also support the company using a Future Fund convertible loan note will not lose relief on any previous EIS investments when that loan is redeemed or converted into shares. The Future Fund was set up as part of Government support to companies impacted by the 2020 coronavirus pandemic and was open to applications up to 31 March 2021 (see www.gov.uk/guidance/future-fund). See **24.14, 24.19** ENTERPRISE INVESTMENT SCHEME and **60.38** ENTERPRISE INVESTMENT SCHEME.

Non-statutory clearances

Applications should be made by email to nonstatutoryclearanceteam.hmrc@hmrc.gsi.gov.uk. See **30.4** HMRC — ADMINISTRATION.

Payment of tax

Self-assessment taxpayers with a payment due on 31 January 2021 of up to £30,000 can use a self-service time to pay facility in order to agree a plan with HMRC to spread their payment over 12 months. The taxpayer must have filed their 2019/20 return, have no other tax debts and have no other payment plans set up. Taxpayers with a payment due in excess of £30,000 must apply for a time to pay arrangement in the usual way. See **51.7** PAYMENT OF TAX.

Penalties and reasonable excuse

A taxpayer's inability to meet an obligation such as a payment date or filing deadline due to coronavirus (COVID-19) will be accepted as a reasonable excuse. However, this is on condition that the taxpayer remedies the failure as soon as they are able to do so. Additionally, taxpayers will need to explain how they were affected by coronavirus when making their appeal. See **42.7** LATE PAYMENT INTEREST AND PENALTIES, **52.2, 52.5** PENALTIES.

Introduction to capital gains tax [1.5]

HMRC have suspended late filing penalties in respect of UK land disposal returns (see 58.21 RETURNS) in respect of disposals that are completed between 6 April 2020 and 30 June 2020, provided that the return is filed by 31 July 2020. See 52.5 PENALTIES.

HMRC will not charge late filing penalties for 2019/20 returns if the return is filed online by 28 February 2021 (HMRC Press Notice 25 January 2021).

HMRC will also not charge the first 5% late payment penalty on income tax and/or capital gains tax due on 31 January 2021 if payment is made, or a time to pay plan set up, by 1 April 2021 (HMRC Press Notice 19 February 2021).

Statutory residence test

The statutory residence test is amended by *FA 2020, s 109* with the effect that days between 1 March 2020 and 1 June 2020 inclusive spent by individuals in the UK for specified reasons connected with the detection, treatment or prevention of coronavirus do not count towards the relevant tests.

This special measure applies for the purposes of determining:

- whether an individual was or was not resident in the UK for 2019/20; and
- if an individual was not resident in the UK for 2019/20 (including the case where the individual's non-resident status was as a result of the special measure), whether the individual is or is not resident in the UK for 2020/21.

See 57.2 RESIDENCE AND DOMICILE.

Key points on the charge to capital gains tax

[1.5] The simplest tax planning ideas can be very effective. Whenever advising on capital gains tax consider whether a potential gain can be:

- split over two tax years to utilise two annual exempt amounts/the remainder of the basic rate band;
- delayed in whole or part until after 6 April/next accounting period to provide a cash flow advantage in terms of payment of tax;
- split between spouses or civil partners to utilise two annual exempt amounts and the remainder of basic rate bands;
- offset by capital losses brought forward; always ask new clients and old accountants about any brought forward capital losses as they are often missed;
- offset by current year capital losses; consider any potential unrealised losses including assets held by any spouse (civil partner) or connected companies;
- offset by any trade tax losses;
- made to qualify for business asset disposal relief, investors' relief or substantial shareholdings exemption;

[1.5] Introduction to capital gains tax

- made to qualify in whole or part for deferral by reinvestment;
- potentially qualify for any other capital gains deduction or relief such as private residence relief, EIS, SEIS and double tax relief.

Other tax planning can centre on whether 'income' can be converted to a capital gain (taxable at 0%, 10%, 18%, 20% or 28%). For example, profits are rolled up in a limited company until the end of a venture when the company is sold or wound up realising a capital gain. Assuming the gain qualifies for entrepreneurs' relief, it will be taxed at 10% compared to profits being extracted via dividends liable to higher rates of income tax.

2
Annual Rates and Exemptions

Rates of tax	2.1
Rates of CGT for individuals	2.1
Rate of CGT for personal representatives	2.2
Rate of CGT for settlements	2.3
Rate of tax on capital gains for companies	2.4
Annual exempt amount	2.5
Annual exempt amount for 2019/20 onwards	2.5
Annual exempt amount for 2018/19 and earlier years	2.6
Key points on annual rates and exemptions	2.7

Rates of tax

Rates of CGT for individuals

[2.1] There are four rates of capital gains tax which may apply to gains: 10%, 18%, 20% and 28%.

Where gains qualify for business asset disposal relief (formerly entrepreneurs' relief) or investors' relief and a claim is made for relief, the rate of tax is **10%**. See **10.8** BUSINESS ASSET DISPOSAL RELIEF and **40.2** INVESTORS' RELIEF. In other cases the rate depends on the type of asset disposed of and on the level of the individual's taxable income for the year.

Upper rate gains

The following applies where the taxpayer's gains for the tax year consist entirely of 'upper rate gains' or entirely of such gains and gains to which entrepreneurs' relief or investors' relief applies. Where the taxpayer's taxable income exceeds the basic rate limit (so that part of his income is taxable at the higher rate, default higher rate, savings higher rate or dividend upper rate — but see below for application to Scottish and Welsh taxpayers), the rate of capital gains tax on the upper rate gains is 28%. In other cases, the rate is 18% on any part of the upper rate gains that does not exceed the 'unused part of the basic rate band' for the year, and the 28% rate applies to any excess. The unused part of the basic rate band is set first against gains which are charged to tax at 10% as a result of an entrepreneurs' relief or investors' relief claim.

An individual's *'unused part of the basic rate band'* for this purpose is the amount by which basic rate limit (£37,700 for 2021/22) exceeds the 'Step 3 income' for the year. The *'Step 3 income'* is the net income less allowances deducted at Step 3 of the calculation in *ITA 2007, s 23* (calculation of income tax liability).

[2.1] Annual Rates and Exemptions

The basic rate limit for earlier years was as follows:

2020/21	£37,500
2019/20	£37,500
2018/19	£34,500
2017/18	£33,500

'*Upper rate gains*' are:

- 'residential property gains' (see below);
- for disposals before 6 April 2019, NRCGT gains (i.e. gains by non-residents on disposals of interests in UK residential property — see **41.31** LAND); and
- 'carried interest gains'.

'*Carried interest gains*' are:

- gains accruing under *TCGA 1992, s 103KA(2)(3)* (carried interest — see **50.19** PARTNERSHIPS); and
- gains accruing to an individual as a result of carried interest arising to him where he performs investment management services directly or indirectly in respect of an investment scheme under arrangements not involving a partnership and the carried interest arises under the arrangements and does not constitute a 'co-investment' repayment or return (see **50.19** PARTNERSHIPS).

Other gains

The following applies where the taxpayer's gains for the tax year consist entirely of gains other than upper rate gains or entirely of such gains and gains to which entrepreneurs' relief applies. Where the taxpayer's taxable income exceeds the basic rate limit, the rate of capital gains tax is 20%. In other cases, the rate is 10% on any part of the gains that does not exceed the unused part of the basic rate band for the year, and the 20% rate applies to any excess. The unused part of the basic rate band is set first against gains which are charged to tax at 10% as a result of an entrepreneurs' relief or investors' relief claim.

Upper rate gains and other gains accrued in same tax year

Where an individual makes both upper rate gains and other gains in the same tax year and his taxable income exceeds the basic rate limit, the rate of tax is 28% or 20% as appropriate. In other cases, the rate is 10% or 18% on any part of the gains that does not exceed the unused part of the basic rate band for the year, and the 20% or 28% rate applies to any excess. The taxpayer may choose which gains are to be allocated to the unused part of the basic rate band (and therefore charged at the 10% or 18% rates), but only after allocating any gains charged to tax at 10% as a result of an entrepreneurs' relief or investors' relief claim.

[*TCGA 1992, ss 1H(1)–(4)(9)–(11), 1I, 1J(1)(7); FA 2019, s 5(1), Sch 1 paras 2, 120*].

Note that, for 2018/19 and earlier years, the above provisions were at *TCGA 1992, ss 4, 4BA*.

Annual Rates and Exemptions [2.1]

Devolution of income tax

For the purposes of the above provisions, an individual who is a Scottish taxpayer is treated as if he were not a Scottish taxpayer i.e. the basic rate band for the rest of the UK (£37,700 for 2021/22) is used above when calculating capital gains tax and *not* the Scottish rate bands. This means, for example, that a Scottish taxpayer paying Scottish higher rate income tax on his non-savings income exceeding the Scottish intermediate rate band, could still pay some capital gains tax at lower rates if within the basic rate band for the rest of the UK. See Tolley's Income Tax for details of the devolution of income tax. [*TCGA 1992, ss 1J(6), 4(10)(11); FA 2019, Sch 1 paras 2, 120*].

Similarly, for 2019/20 onwards, an individual who is a Welsh taxpayer is treated as if he were not a Welsh taxpayer. [*TCGA 1992, s 1J(6); FA 2019, Sch 1 paras 2, 120*].

Special cases

Where:

(a) under *ITTOIA 2005, s 539* (gains from contracts for life insurance etc.), a person is entitled to relief by reference to the amount of a deficiency, or

(b) under *ITTOIA 2005, s 669(1)(2)* (reduction in residuary income: inheritance tax on accrued income) the residuary income of an estate is treated as reduced so as to reduce a person's income by any amount for the purposes of extra liability,

the person's Step 3 income for the year is treated (for the purpose only of computing the unused part of the basic rate band) as reduced by the amount of the deficiency or, as the case may be, the amount in (b) above. The Step 3 income cannot be reduced below zero (*Scott v HMRC* CA, [2020] STC 353).

Where under *ITTOIA 2005, s 465* (gains from contracts for life insurance etc.) a person's total income for the year is deemed to include any amount(s):

(i) in determining the unused part of the basic rate band, his Step 3 income is treated as including not the whole of the amount(s) concerned but only the annual equivalent within the meaning of *ITTOIA 2005, s 536(1)* or (as the case may be) the total annual equivalent within the meaning of *ITTOIA 2005, s 537*, and

(ii) if relief is given under *ITTOIA 2005, s 535* and the calculation under *s 536(1)* or *s 537* does not involve the higher rate of income tax, the capital gains tax rate is determined as if the person's taxable income does not exceed the basic rate limit as described above.

[*TCGA 1992, s 1J(2)–(5)(7)(8); FA 2019, Sch 1 para 2*]. Note that, for 2018/19 and earlier years, these provisions were at *TCGA 1992, s 4A*.

Deduction of losses and annual exempt amount

Losses may be used in the most beneficial way, and so may be deducted from a gain irrespective of the rate of tax which would otherwise apply. They can only be deducted from a gain so far as necessary to eliminate the gain. The taxpayer can also deduct the annual exempt amount (see **2.5** below) in the most beneficial way. This latter rule is, however, subject to any provision limiting the way in which losses can be deducted (for example where a loss is made on a disposal to a connected person — see **44.7** LOSSES) and, for 2018/19 and earlier years, applies only if gains for the year are chargeable at different rates.

It will be most beneficial to set losses and the annual exempt amount against gains chargeable at 28% before those chargeable at 20%, against those chargeable at 20% before those chargeable at 18% and so on.

[*TCGA 1992, ss 1F(1)–(3), 1K(5); FA 2019, Sch 1 para 2*]. Note that, for 2018/19 and earlier years, these provisions were at *TCGA 1992, s 4B*.

Residential property gain

The legislation defining a 'residential property gain' has been rewritten for disposals in 2019/20 onwards. For such disposals, a single definition applies, regardless of where the land in question is situated. Previously, separate definitions applied to UK and non-UK land (although the two definitions had similar effect).

2019/20 onwards

For 2019/20 onwards, a '*residential property gain*' is so much of a chargeable gain on a 'disposal of residential property' as is attributable to that property. The proportion so attributable is equal to the number of days in the 'applicable period' on which the land consists of or includes a 'dwelling' divided by the total number of days in the applicable period. If there has been 'mixed use' of the land on one or more of the days in the applicable period, the proportion must be adjusted, on a just and reasonable basis, to take account of the mixed use.

The '*applicable period*' is the period beginning with the day on which the interest in land being disposed of was acquired (or 31 March 1982 if later) and ending the day before the day of the disposal. If the interest disposed of is in UK land and the person making the disposal is not UK-resident (or the disposal is made in the overseas part of a tax year which is split under the statutory residence test), the applicable period begins on 6 April 2015 if that date is later than the date on which the interest was acquired. There is 'mixed use' of land on any day on which it consists of both one or more dwellings and other land.

If the disposal is of an interest in land which subsists under a contract for an off-plan purchase, i.e. a contract for acquisition of land consisting of, or including, a building or part of a building that is to be constructed or adapted as a dwelling, the land is treated as consisting of, or including, a dwelling throughout the applicable period. Where the interest disposed of results from interests which have been acquired at different times, the date of acquisition of the first interest is taken as the date on which all the interests were acquired.

There is a '*disposal of residential property*' on a disposal of an 'interest in land' if the land consisted of or included a dwelling at any time in the applicable period; if the interest in land subsisted for the benefit of land consisting of or including a dwelling at any time in the applicable period or if the interest subsisted under a contract for an off-plan purchase. The grant of an option (defined as at **7.7** ASSETS) binding the grantor to sell an interest in land is treated for these purposes as the disposal of an interest in land.

Annual Rates and Exemptions [2.1]

An '*interest in land*' is an estate, interest, right or power in or over land, or the benefit of an obligation, restriction or condition affecting the value of such, but not including:

- any interest or right (other than a rentcharge or, in Scotland, a feu duty) held to secure payment of money or performance of any other obligation; or
- a licence to use or occupy land;
- in England, Wales or Northern Ireland, a tenancy at will or an advowson, franchise (i.e. a grant from the Crown, such as the right to hold a market or fair, or the right to take tolls) or manor; or
- any other interest or right specified in Treasury regulations.

In the case of non-UK land, the domestic legal concepts mentioned above must be read so as to produce the result most closely corresponding with that produced in relation to UK land.

A '*dwelling*' is a building (including a part of a building) which is used or suitable for use as a dwelling or is in the process of being constructed or adapted for such use. It includes gardens and grounds (and any building or structure in a garden or grounds). The following are excluded from being a dwelling:

- school residential accommodation;
- residential accommodation for members of the armed forces;
- homes or institutions providing residential accommodation for children;
- homes or institutions providing residential accommodation with personal care for the elderly, the disabled, persons with drug or alcohol dependency or a mental disorder;
- hospitals and hospices;
- prisons and similar establishments;
- hotels, inns and similar establishments;
- any other institution which is the sole or main residence of its residents; and
- buildings occupied by students managed or controlled by their educational establishments (within *Housing Act 2004, Sch 14 para 4* or corresponding Scottish or NI provision).

In addition, a building which includes at least 15 bedrooms, is purpose-built or converted for occupation by students other than school pupils and is occupied by them for at least 165 days in a tax year is not a dwelling for that year.

Buildings which become temporarily unsuitable for use as a dwelling are generally treated as continuing to be such, but there are some exceptions. A building is not considered suitable for use as a dwelling if the temporary unsuitability resulted from damage to the building which was accidental, or otherwise outside the control of the person making the disposal and the period of temporary unsuitability was at least 90 days (whether or not within the applicable period but ending before the disposal). If this is the case, any work done within that period is not treated as construction or adaptation of the building for use as a dwelling. Any damage occurring during alterations to, or partial demolition of, a building which involved, or could be expected to

[2.1] Annual Rates and Exemptions

involve, the building being unsuitable for use as a dwelling for at least 30 days is not considered accidental or otherwise outside the control of the person making the disposal for these purposes.

A building which has been demolished either to ground level or, in accordance with planning permission or development consent, to a single facade (double if on a corner) is regarded as having ceased to exist. Where a person disposes of an interest in land which contains or contained a building which has been suitable for use as a dwelling and that building has undergone works which result in it ceasing to exist or becoming unsuitable as a dwelling before the 'completion' of disposal then the building is treated as being unsuitable as a dwelling throughout the period when the works were in progress, and any period ending immediately before that during which the building was, for reasons connected with the works, not used as a dwelling. This rule applies only if the works are *'qualifying works'*, i.e. where any planning permission or development consent required for the works or any change or use with which they are associated has been granted (even if retrospectively after completion of the disposal) and the works were carried out in accordance with it. If, at any time when qualifying works were in progress, the building was undergoing any other work for which planning permission or development consent was required but not granted (unless given subsequently), or it was contravened, the building is not treated as being unsuitable as a dwelling during that time. If works are not qualifying works at the completion of the disposal, they do not affect the building's suitability as a dwelling at any time before the disposal.

'*Completion*' occurs either at the time of disposal or, where the contract is completed by conveyance, transfer or other instrument, when the instrument takes effect.

The Treasury may by regulations amend the definition of 'dwelling'.

[TCGA 1992, Sch 1B; FA 2019, Sch 1 paras 15, 120].

2018/19 and earlier years

For 2018/19 and earlier years, a '*residential property gain*' or loss is a gain or loss (computed as below) on the disposal of a residential property interest, being either a 'disposal of a UK residential property interest' or a 'disposal of a non-UK residential property interest' but excluding a gain or loss on a non-resident CGT disposal (see **41.31** LAND). A '*disposal of a UK residential property interest*' is defined as at **41.35** LAND but the reference there to 6 April 2015 is replaced for this purpose by a reference to 31 March 1982.

A '*disposal of a non-UK residential property interest*' is a disposal of an 'interest in non-UK land' which has, at any time in the period from acquisition or, if later, 31 March 1982 to the day before the date of disposal (the '*relevant period of ownership*'), consisted of or included a 'dwelling', or which subsists for the benefit of land that has consisted of or included a dwelling at any time in that period. Alternatively it is a disposal of an interest in non-UK land which subsists under a contract for an off-plan purchase, i.e. a contract for acquisition of land consisting of, or including, a building or part of a building that is to be constructed or adapted as a dwelling. In determining the period of ownership, where the interest disposed of results from interests which have been acquired at different times, the date of acquisition of the first interest is taken as the date on which all the interests were acquired. The grant of an option (defined as at 7.7 ASSETS) binding the grantor to sell an interest in non-UK land is treated for these purposes as the disposal of an interest in non-UK land.

An '*interest in non-UK land*' is an estate, interest, right or power in or over land outside the UK, or the benefit of an obligation, restriction or condition affecting the value of such, but not including:

(a) any interest or right held to secure payment of money or performance of any other obligation; or
(b) a licence to use or occupy land.

A '*dwelling*' is a building (including a part of a building) which is used or suitable for use as a dwelling or is in the process of being constructed or adapted for such use. It includes gardens and grounds (and any building or structure in a garden or grounds). The following are excluded from being a dwelling:

(i)   school residential accommodation;
(ii)   residential accommodation for members of the armed forces;
(iii) homes or institutions providing residential accommodation for children;
(iv)   homes or institutions providing residential accommodation with personal care for the elderly, the disabled, persons with drug or alcohol dependency or a mental disorder;
(v)   hospitals and hospices;
(vi)   prisons and similar establishments;
(vii) hotels, inns and similar establishments; and
(viii) any other institution which is the sole or main residence of its residents.

In addition, a building which includes at least 15 bedrooms, is purpose-built or converted for occupation by students other than school pupils and is occupied by them for at least 165 days in a tax year is not a dwelling for that year.

Buildings which become temporarily unsuitable for use as a dwelling are generally treated as continuing to be such, but there are some exceptions. A building is not considered suitable for use as a dwelling if the temporary unsuitability resulted from damage to the building which was accidental, or otherwise outside the control of the person making the disposal and the period of temporary unsuitability was at least 90 days (whether or not within the relevant period of ownership but ending before the disposal). If this is the case any work done within that period is not treated as construction or adaptation of the building for use as a dwelling. Any damage occurring during alterations to, or partial demolition of, a building which involved, or could be expected to involve, the building being unsuitable for use as a dwelling for at least 30 days is not considered accidental or otherwise outside the control of the person making the disposal for these purposes.

A building which has been demolished either to ground level or, in accordance with planning permission or development consent, to a single façade (double if on a corner) is regarded as having ceased to exist. Where a person disposes of an interest in non-UK land which contains or contained a building which has been suitable for use as a dwelling at any time in the relevant period of ownership, and that building has undergone complete or partial demolition or other works which result in it ceasing to exist or becoming unsuitable as a dwelling before the 'completion' of disposal then, provided the conditions below are met, the building is treated as being unsuitable as a dwelling throughout the period when the works were in progress, and any period ending immediately before that during which the building was, for reasons connected with the works, not used as a dwelling. The conditions are that:

- the works result in the building ceasing to exist or becoming unsuitable as a dwelling before the completion of the disposal; and
- any planning permission or development consent has been issued (even if retrospectively after completion of the disposal) and the works were carried out in accordance with it.

If planning permission or development consent for the works was required but not granted (unless given subsequently), or it was contravened, the building is not treated as being unsuitable as a dwelling.

'*Completion*' occurs either at the time of disposal or when the interest is conveyed where the contract is completed by conveyance.

The Treasury may by regulations exclude any other interest or right from being treated as an interest in non-UK land and amend the definition of 'dwelling'.

[TCGA 1992, Sch BA1; FA 2019, Sch 1 paras 11, 120].

2018/19 and earlier years — computation of residential property gain

The following rules apply to determine how much of a gain arising before 6 April 2019 on a disposal of a residential property interest (an '*RPI disposal*') is a residential property gain and therefore is taxable as an upper rate gain. The rules apply equally to losses but do not apply to non-resident CGT disposals (for which see **41.36, 41.37** LAND).They apply to the disposal of contracts for off-plan purchases (see above) as if the interest consisted of (or included) a dwelling throughout the period in which the taxpayer owned it.

Default method

This method applies if the RPI disposal is not, and does not involve, a high value disposal of dwellings within **15.12** COMPANIES. The gain or loss is calculated in the normal way and is then apportioned by the fraction:

$$\frac{RD}{TD}$$

where RD is the number of days in the relevant period of ownership on which the disposed of interest consisted wholly or partly of a dwelling (defined as above for non-UK interests and as at **41.35** LAND for UK interests); and TD is the number of days in that period.

The resulting gain or loss is the residential property gain or loss.

Where there are any days in the relevant period of ownership on which the land disposed of consists partly but not exclusively of one or more dwellings (i.e. there is '*mixed use*') a just and reasonable apportionment must be made to calculate the residential property gain or loss.

Annual Rates and Exemptions [2.1]

Any remaining part of the actual gain or loss on the RPI disposal after deducting the residential property gain or loss is not a residential property gain or loss.

Method where disposal involves a high value disposal

Where an RPI disposal by a company is, or involves, one or more high value disposals of dwellings within **15.12** COMPANIES the residential property gain or loss is the sum of the residential property gains or losses accruing on each such high value disposal calculated as described below. Where part only of the land disposed of is such a high value disposal, the remaining part of the land is treated for these purposes in the same way as if it formed part of the high value disposal. Where there are any days in the ownership period in question on which the land disposed of consists partly but not exclusively of one or more dwellings (i.e. there is '*mixed use*') a just and reasonable apportionment must be made to calculate the residential property gain or loss on the non-high value disposal. The balancing gain or loss on the RPI disposal is the sum of the balancing gains or losses for each high value disposal.

(1) **High value disposal not within Cases 1–3 or where an election is made.** Where the high value disposal does not fall within any of Cases 1–3 or an election for the retrospective basis of computation is made (see **15.12** COMPANIES), the residential property gain or loss arising on the high value disposal is the fraction of the actual gain or loss on that disposal found by applying:

$$\frac{SD}{TD}$$

where SD is the number of days in the relevant period of ownership on which the interest disposed of consisted wholly or partly of a dwelling but which was not an ATED chargeable day (see **15.12** COMPANIES); and TD is the total number of days in that period.

The amount of the gain or loss which is neither ATED-related nor a residential property gain or loss in these circumstances is the balancing gain or loss. It is found by applying the fraction:

$$\frac{BD}{TD}$$

where BD is the number of days in the relevant period of ownership which are neither days on which the interest disposed of consisted wholly or partly of a dwelling but was not an ATED chargeable day nor ATED chargeable days, and

TD is the number of days in that period.

(2) **High value disposal within Cases 1–3 and no election made.** Where the high value disposal falls within any of Cases 1–3 at **15.12** COMPANIES and no election for the retrospective basis of computation is made (see **15.12** COMPANIES), the residential property gain or loss is the sum of a propor-

17

tion of the 'notional post-ATED gain' and a proportion of the 'notional pre-ATED gain or loss'. The proportion of the notional post-ATED gain or loss is that given by the fraction:

$$\frac{SD}{TD}$$

where SD is the number of days in the period from 6 April in the 'relevant year' to the day before the date of disposal on which the interest disposed of consisted wholly or partly of a dwelling but which was not an ATED chargeable day, and
TD is the total number of days in that period.
The proportion of the notional pre-ATED gain or loss is that given by the fraction:

$$\frac{SD}{TD}$$

where SD is the number of days in the period from the date of acquisition, or 31 March 1982 if later, to 5 in the relevant year, on which the interest disposed of consisted wholly or partly of a dwelling but which was not an ATED chargeable day, and TD is the total number of days in that period.
The '*notional post-ATED gain or loss*' is the notional gain or loss on the disposal of the disposed of interest had the company acquired it at market value on 5 April in the relevant year. In calculating the notional post-ATED gain or loss the assumption that the interest was acquired on 5 April of the relevant year is ignored when determining whether the interest is a WASTING ASSET (**72**).*TCGA 1992, s 41* (restriction of losses by reference to capital allowances: see **17.14** COMPUTATION OF GAINS AND LOSSES) and *TCGA 1992, s 47* (wasting assets qualifying for capital allowances: see **72.2** WASTING ASSETS) apply in relation to any capital or renewals allowance made in respect of the expenditure actually incurred in acquiring or providing the asset as if that allowance were made in respect of the expenditure treated as incurred on the deemed acquisition date.
The '*notional pre-ATED gain or loss*' is that which would have accrued on 5 April of the relevant year if the interest had been disposed of at market value on that date.
The '*relevant year*' is 2013 where Case 1 applies, 2015 where Case 2 applies or 2016 where Case 3 applies.
The amount of the gain or loss which is neither ATED-related nor a residential property gain or loss in these circumstances is the balancing gain or loss. This is the sum of the balancing gain or loss belonging to the notional post-ATED gain or loss and the balancing gain or loss belonging to the notional pre-ATED gain or loss. These are the fraction of the gains or losses relating to the days in the appropriate period which are

Annual Rates and Exemptions [2.1]

neither days on which the interest disposed of consisted wholly or partly of a dwelling but were not an ATED chargeable day nor ATED chargeable days.

[TCGA 1992, s 57C, Sch 4ZZC; FA 2019, Sch 1 paras 7, 20, 120].

Example 1

Erica owns an established business and has taxable profits of £42,270 for her accounting year ended 5 April 2022. She has no other income for 2021/22 but she makes a chargeable gain (before deduction of the annual exempt amount) of £30,300. The gain is not an upper rate gain and does not qualify for business asset disposal relief. Her capital gains tax liability for 2021/22 is computed as follows.

	£
Trade profits	42,270
Deduct Personal allowance	12,570
Step 3 income	£29,700
Unused part of the basic rate band (£37,700 – £29,700)	£8,000
Chargeable gain	30,300
Deduct Annual exempt amount (see **2.6** below)	12,300
Taxable gain	£18,000

£		£
8,000	@ 10%	800
10,000	@ 20%	2,000
£18,000		£2,800

Example 2

Felix owns an established business and has taxable profits of £42,500 for his accounting year ended 31 March 2022. He has no other income for 2021/22 but he makes two chargeable gains (before deducting the annual exempt amount) of £17,000 each. Neither gain is an upper rate gain but one of them qualifies for business asset disposal relief. His capital gains tax liability for 2021/22 is computed as follows.

Disposal qualifying for business asset disposal relief

	£
Capital gains tax £17,000 × 10%	£1,700
Disposal not qualifying for business asset disposal relief	
Chargeable gain	17,000
Deduct Annual exempt amount (see **2.6** below)	12,300
Taxable gain	£4,700
Capital gains tax £4,700 × 20%	£940
Total capital gains tax for 2021/22 (£1,700 + £940)	£2,640

[2.1] Annual Rates and Exemptions

Notes to the example

(a) Gains qualifying for business asset disposal relief are treated as the lowest part of the gains for the year. The unused part of the basic rate band (£7,770) is set against the gain qualifying for business asset disposal relief even though it does not affect the rate of tax for that gain. The whole of the gain not qualifying for business asset disposal relief is therefore chargeable to tax at 20%.

(b) It is assumed that Felix sets his annual exempt amount against the gain chargeable at 20% as this achieves the greater tax saving.

Example 3

Marley owns an established business and has taxable profits of £42,770 for her accounting year ended 31 March 2022. She has no other income for 2021/22 but she makes two chargeable gains (before deducting the annual exempt amount) of £17,000 each. Neither gain qualifies for business asset disposal relief but one of them is an upper rate gain. Her capital gains tax liability for 2021/22 is computed as follows.

	£
Trade profits	42,770
Deduct Personal allowance	12,570
Step 3 income	£30,200
Unused part of the basic rate band (£37,700 – £30,200)	£7,500

Standard rate gain

£			£
7,500	@ 10%		750
9,500	@ 20%		1,900
£17,000			£2,650

Upper rate gain

	£
Chargeable gain	17,000
Deduct Annual exempt amount (see **2.6** below)	12,300
Taxable gain	£4,700
Capital gains tax £4,700 × 28%	£1,316
Total capital gains tax for 2020/21 (£2,650 + £1,316)	£3,966

Notes to the example

(a) The taxpayer can choose to set the unused part of the basic rate band (£7,500) against either the upper rate gain or the other gain. In practice the effect is the same as there is a 10% reduction in the rate of CGT applicable to the gain falling within the unused part of the band. In this example the unused part is set against the standard rate gain for illustration purposes.

(b) It is assumed that Marley sets her annual exempt amount against the gain chargeable at 28% as this achieves the greater tax saving.

Rate of CGT for personal representatives

[2.2] The rate of tax is 28% for upper rate gains (see **2.1** above) and 20% for other gains. [*TCGA 1992, ss 1H(5)(6), 4(3); FA 2019, Sch 1 para 2*]. Where it is necessary to determine from which chargeable gains a loss may be deducted or which losses are to be deducted from a chargeable gain, the losses may be used in the most beneficial way. [*TCGA 1992, ss 1F(1), 4B; FA 2019, Sch 1 para 2*].

Rate of CGT for settlements

[2.3] See SETTLEMENTS (**62.7**).

Rate of tax on capital gains for companies

[2.4] Companies and other corporate bodies within the charge to corporation tax do not pay capital gains tax as such. Instead they are chargeable to corporation tax on their chargeable gains. The whole of a company's gains for an accounting period (net of allowable losses) are included in the profits chargeable to corporation tax.

For disposals before 6 April 2019, there were two exceptions to the rule that companies do not pay capital gains tax. The exceptions were for the capital gains tax charges on high value disposals of dwellings (see **15.12** COMPANIES) and non-resident disposals of UK residential property interests (see **41.31** LAND). For later disposals, the charge on high value disposals of dwellings is abolished and the charge on UK residential property interests is replaced by the corporation tax charge on disposals of interests in UK land by non-residents (see **41.23** LAND). See **15.3** COMPANIES.

Annual exempt amount

Annual exempt amount for 2019/20 onwards

[2.5] For 2020/21 and 2021/22, an individual who has chargeable gains for the year can deduct the annual exempt amount of **£12,300** from those gains (but no further than is needed to reduce them to nil). (The annual exempt amount is sometimes referred to as the 'annual exemption'.) For 2019/20, the annual exempt amount was £12,000. The annual exempt amount is to remain at £12,300 for 2022/23 to 2025/26 inclusive.

The annual exempt amount is deducted after deducting allowable losses of the same tax year, but before deducting any allowable losses brought forward from previous tax years or carried back from the tax year of death (see **20.7** DEATH). The taxpayer can deduct the annual exempt amount in the most beneficial way.

An individual who makes a claim under *ITA 2007, s 809B* for the remittance basis to apply for a tax year (see **55.2** REMITTANCE BASIS) is not entitled to the annual exempt amount for that year. The annual exempt amount cannot be deducted from foreign gains arising in one year and chargeable in a later tax year in which they are remitted to the UK.

[2.5] Annual Rates and Exemptions

These provisions also apply to personal representatives for the year of death and the following two years (see **20.9** DEATH).

The exempt amount for a tax year, unless Parliament determines otherwise, is the previous year's exempt amount as increased by a percentage which is the same as the percentage increase in the consumer prices index for the September preceding the tax year over the index for the previous September. The resulting figure is rounded up to the nearest £100 and is announced before the relevant tax year in a Treasury statutory instrument. If there is no such increase in the index, the previous year's exempt amount is used for the next year without the need for a statutory instrument (unless Parliament determines otherwise). Increases under this rule have been disapplied for 2021/22 to 2025/26 inclusive.

[TCGA 1992, ss 1K, 1L; FA 2019, Sch 1 paras 2, 120; FA 2021, s 40; SI 2020 No 333].

Examples

For 2021/22, Pablo, who is resident in the UK, has chargeable gains of £14,500 and allowable losses of £1,200. He also has allowable losses of £14,000 brought forward.

	£
Net gains (£14,500–£1,200)	13,300
Annual exempt amount	12,300
	1,000
Losses brought forward (part)	1,000
Taxable gains	Nil
Losses brought forward	14,000
Less utilised in 2021/22	1,000
Losses carried forward	£13,000

For 2021/22, Maria (who is also UK-resident) has the same gains and losses (including brought-forward losses) as Pablo above, but is also a beneficiary of an offshore trust. Trust gains of £12,600 are attributed to her for 2021/22 under TCGA 1992, s 87.

	£
Gains (£14,500 + £12,600)	27,100
Deduct current year loss	1,200
	25,900
Deduct Annual exempt amount	(12,300)
	13,600
Deduct Losses brought forward (part)	(13,300)
Taxable gains*	£300
Losses brought forward	14,000
Less utilised in 2021/22	13,300

Losses carried forward	£700

* Attributed gains cannot be covered by personal losses. The exempt amount is therefore allocated to attributed gains in priority to personal gains as this results in the greatest reduction in taxable gains. £300 (£12,600 – £12,300) of the attributed gains remain taxable.

Annual exempt amount for 2018/19 and earlier years

[2.6] For 2018/19, an individual is exempt from capital gains tax on the first £11,700 of his 'taxable amount'. This amount is known as the 'annual exempt amount' or sometimes, the 'annual exemption'. For 2017/18, the annual exempt amount was £11,300.

Where an individual makes a claim under *ITA 2007, s 809B* (see **55.2** REMITTANCE BASIS) for the remittance basis to apply for a tax year, however, he is not entitled to the annual exempt amount for that year.

The *'taxable amount'* is the amount on which the individual is chargeable to capital gains tax (including any gains treated under *TCGA 1992, s 86* as accruing to him as settlor from a non-UK resident settlement in which he has an interest (see **48.5** OFFSHORE SETTLEMENTS)) after deducting allowable losses for the year or UK part and brought-forward allowable losses, plus any gains treated under *TCGA 1992, s 87* or *s 89(2)* as accruing to him as a beneficiary of a non-UK resident settlement (an offshore trust) (see **48.13–48.20** OFFSHORE SETTLEMENTS).

Where an individual's 'adjusted net gains' are equal to or less than the annual exempt amount, any allowable losses brought forward from a previous year or carried back from the year of death (see **20.7** DEATH) need not be deducted and are thus preserved for further carry-forward (or, if possible, carry-back). Where the 'adjusted net gains' exceed the annual exempt amount, such losses are deducted only to the extent necessary to wipe out the excess.

The *'adjusted net gains'* are:

(i) where the taxpayer is resident in the UK for the tax year and the year is not a split year under the statutory residence test (see **57.17** RESIDENCE AND DOMICILE), the chargeable gains for the year (including gains attributed under *TCGA 1992, s 86*) *less* any current year allowable losses. Where *TCGA 1992, s 16ZB* (now *TCGA 1992, Sch 1 para 2*) applies (gains charged on REMITTANCE BASIS (**55.2**)), the 'relevant gains' within that section are deducted from the chargeable gains for the year before deducting current year losses. Where gains are attributed under *TCGA 1992, ss 87, 87L, 87K* or *89(2)*, such gains are also included in the adjusted net gains to the extent that they do not exceed the annual exempt amount (and will thus be covered by that amount);

(ii) where the taxpayer is not resident in the UK during any part of a tax year, the gains realised for the year on UK residential property falling within the non-resident CGT regime that applies for disposals made on or after 6 April 2015, reduced by losses realised under the same regime for that year (not including losses brought forward) (see **41.31** LAND);

[2.6] Annual Rates and Exemptions

(iii) where the taxpayer is resident in the UK for the tax year and the year is a split year, the total amount of the gains in (i) and (ii) above.

These provisions also apply to personal representatives for the year of death and the following two years (see **20.9** DEATH).

[*TCGA 1992, ss 2(2), 3(1)(2)(5)–(5D)(7); SI 2018 No 244*].

Where a taxpayer is chargeable to capital gains tax at more than one rate, he may allocate the annual exempt amount (and any allowable losses) against gains in the most tax-efficient way. See **2.1** above.

The exempt amount for the year, unless Parliament determines otherwise, is the previous year's exempt amount as increased by a percentage which is the same as the percentage increase in the consumer prices index for the September preceding the year of assessment over the index for the previous September. The resulting figure is rounded up to the nearest £100 and is announced before the relevant year of assessment in a Treasury statutory instrument (see list of references above). If there is no such increase in the relevant index, the previous year's exempt amount is used for the next year without the need for a statutory instrument (unless Parliament determines otherwise). [*ITA 2007, s 989; TCGA 1992, ss 3(2A)–(4), 288(2)*].

See **62.8** and **62.9** SETTLEMENTS for further applications of the above rules.

The annual exempt amount is available regardless of the residence status of the individual and is available separately to each spouse or civil partner. See above for the loss of the annual exempt amount where a claim for the remittance basis has been made by a non-UK domiciled individual.

> *Examples*
>
> For 2018/19, Paul, who is resident in the UK, has chargeable gains of £14,200 and allowable losses of £1,200. He also has allowable losses of £14,000 brought forward.
>
> | | £ |
> |---|---:|
> | Adjusted net gains (£14,200 – £1,200) | 13,000 |
> | Losses brought forward (part) | 1,300 |
> | | 11,700 |
> | Annual exempt amount | 11,700 |
> | Taxable gains | Nil |
> | | |
> | Losses brought forward | 14,000 |
> | *Less* utilised in 2018/19 | 1,300 |
> | Losses carried forward | £12,700 |

For 2018/19, Mary (who is also UK-resident) has the same gains and losses (including brought-forward losses) as Paul above, but is also a beneficiary of an offshore trust. Trust gains of £12,000 are attributed to her for 2018/19 under *TCGA 1992, s 87*.

	£
Adjusted net gains (£14,200 – £1,200 + £11,700*)	24,700
Losses brought forward (part)	13,000
	11,700
Annual exempt amount	11,700
	Nil
Add: TCGA 1992, s 87 gains not brought in above	300
Taxable gains	£300
Losses brought forward	14,000
Less utilised in 2018/19	13,000
Losses carried forward	£1,000

* Gains attributed under *TCGA 1992, s 87* are included in adjusted net gains only to the extent that they do not exceed the annual exempt amount. Such gains cannot be covered by personal losses.

For 2018/19, Peter is in the same position as Mary except that his attributed gains are only £6,100.

	£
Adjusted net gains (£14,200 – £1,200 + £6,100)	19,100
Losses brought forward (part)	7,400
	11,700
Annual exempt amount	11,700
Taxable gains	Nil
Losses brought forward	14,000
Less utilised in 2018/19	7,400
Losses carried forward	£6,600

In Peter's case, £6,100 of the annual exempt amount is set against the attributed gains. Losses brought forward are used only to the extent necessary to reduce the personal gains to the balance of the annual exempt amount (£5,600).

[2.6] Annual Rates and Exemptions

Key points on annual rates and exemptions

[2.7] Points to consider are as follows:

- At its lowest level the annual exempt amount is worth £1,230 (12,300 × 10%); at its highest it is worth £3,444 (12,300 × 28%). Significant tax planning therefore revolves around trying to crystallise gains that will be covered by this relief (or multiple annual exempt amounts). For example, the overall tax rate may be reduced where a gain can be split between spouses or civil partners or over two tax years. Also, popular is partially breaking the terms for a relief so a small gain arises (covered by the exemption) whilst the majority of the gain is rolled/held over. For example, adjust the consideration for the transfer such that a gain arises equal to the amount of the annual exempt amount. No tax is payable on the cash proceeds whilst the base cost is increased, reducing the potential gain on a future disposal.
- Business asset disposal relief (formerly entrepreneurs' relief) and investors' relief reduce the rate of capital gains tax to 10% for gains on qualifying disposals of business assets. See **10 BUSINESS ASSET DISPOSAL RELIEF** and **40 INVESTORS' RELIEF**.
- Taxpayers can choose how the annual exempt amount and any allowable losses are allocated against gains. It is normally beneficial to offset these amounts against the gains taxable at the highest rates.
- A taxpayer's basic rate band is extended by qualifying pension contributions and gift aid donations (gross amounts). Certain gift aid donations can be carried back.
- If a taxpayer does not use the annual exempt amount for a tax year, it is wasted: the amount cannot be carried forward or transferred to a spouse or civil partner. Consideration should therefore be given to realising sufficient gains to maximise use of the exemption.
- Spouses and civil partners may consider transferring an asset to the other spouse or partner before disposal in order to benefit from a lower rate of capital gains tax or to utilise their annual exempt amount. However, care is required where the asset potentially qualifies for business asset disposal relief or investors' relief: will the other party also qualify?
- An individual who claims the remittance basis is not entitled to the annual exempt amount for that year.

3

Alternative Finance Arrangements

Introduction to alternative finance arrangements	3.1
Capital gains tax consequences of alternative finance arrangement	3.2
Further consequences for diminishing shared ownership arrangements	3.3
Further consequences for investment bond arrangements	3.4
Investment bond arrangements where the underlying asset is land	3.5

Simon's Taxes. See B5.6.

Introduction to alternative finance arrangements

[3.1] Certain types of finance arrangements (known as *'alternative finance arrangements'*) which are broadly equivalent to loans, deposits etc. but which do not involve the receipt or payment of interest are subject to special tax provisions designed to ensure that they are taxed no more nor less favourably than equivalent products which do involve interest. Such arrangements are usually aimed at those wishing to adhere to Shari'a law, which prohibits the receipt or payment of interest. The tax rules are not, however, restricted to Shari'a-compliant products, but apply to any arrangements falling within their terms.

This chapter describes the tax rules for alternative finance arrangements only to the extent of their effect on capital gains tax. See Tolley's Income Tax and Tolley's Corporation Tax for the detailed provisions.

For corporation tax purposes, the arrangements are loan relationships so that all profits and losses are dealt with as income: see **16.5** COMPANIES — CORPORATE FINANCE AND INTANGIBLES. For capital gains tax purposes, the return on the arrangement that is broadly equivalent to interest is excluded from the consideration for the purchase and sale of the asset purchased under the arrangements.

A further chargeable gains relief applies to certain investment bond arrangements involving land which are equivalent to a securitisation of the land.

The Treasury has the power by statutory instrument to amend the existing provisions, and to introduce new provisions, relating to alternative finance arrangements. [*CTA 2009, s 521; TIOPA 2010, s 366*].

Capital gains tax consequences of alternative finance arrangement

[3.2] Where, under any of three types of alternative finance arrangements, an asset is sold by one party to the arrangements to the other party, the 'alternative finance return' is excluded in determining for capital gains tax purposes the

[3.2] Alternative Finance Arrangements

consideration for the sale and purchase of the asset. This does not affect the operation of any provision providing for the consideration to be treated as an amount other than the actual consideration.

This provision applies to the following types of arrangements: 'purchase and resale arrangements', 'diminishing shared ownership arrangements' and 'investment bond arrangements'. For each type of arrangement there is a particular definition of 'alternative finance return'.

Arrangements which are not at arm's length are not alternative finance arrangements for these purposes if the transfer pricing rules of TIOPA 2010, s 147(3)(5) require the alternative finance return to be recomputed on an arm's length basis and the party receiving the return is not subject to income tax, corporation tax or a corresponding foreign tax on the return.

[TCGA 1992, ss 151O, 151X].

Purchase and resale arrangements

For this purpose, '*purchase and resale arrangements*' are, broadly, arrangements entered into between two persons (A and B), at least one of whom is a 'financial institution' (as defined), under which:

(a) A purchases an asset and sells it to B;
(b) the amount payable by B in respect of the sale (the '*sale price*') is greater than the amount paid by A in respect of the purchase (the 'purchase price');
(c) all or part of the sale price does not have to be paid until a time after the sale; and
(d) the difference between the sale price and the purchase price equates, in substance, to the return on an investment of money at interest.

The sale of the asset in (a) above must take place immediately after the purchase unless A is a financial institution and the asset was purchased by A for the purpose of entering into the arrangements.

The '*alternative finance return*' is so much of the sale price as exceeds the purchase price. If, however, the purchase price is paid by instalments, the alternative finance return in each instalment is the amount of interest which would have been included in the instalment if the purchase price were a loan from A to B, the instalment were a part repayment of principal with interest and the loan were made on arm's length terms and accounted for under generally accepted accounting practice. If the alternative finance return is paid in a currency other than sterling, then if either A or B is not a company and the payment is not made for the purposes of a trade, profession, vocation or property business, the amount of the return is calculated in that currency and then translated into sterling at a spot rate for the day of payment.

[TCGA 1992, ss 151J, 151P, 151Q].

Diminishing shared ownership arrangements

'*Diminishing shared ownership arrangements*' are, broadly, arrangements under which a financial institution acquires a beneficial interest in an asset and another person (the '*eventual owner*'):

(i) also acquires a beneficial interest in the asset;
(ii) is to make payments to the financial institution amounting in aggregate to the consideration paid for the acquisition of its beneficial interest;
(iii) is to acquire (whether or not in stages) the financial institution's beneficial interest as a result of those payments;
(iv) is to make other payments to the financial institution (whether under a lease forming part of the arrangements or otherwise);
(v) has the exclusive right to occupy or otherwise use the asset; and
(vi) is exclusively entitled to any income, profit or gain attributable to the asset (including any increase in its value).

The '*alternative finance return*' is equal to the payments made by the eventual owner under the arrangements other than payments within (ii) above and payments in respect of any arrangement fee or legal or other costs or expenses which the eventual owner is required to pay under the arrangements.

[*TCGA 1992, ss 151K, 151R*].

Investment bond arrangements

'*Investment bond arrangements*' are, broadly, arrangements which:

- provide for one person (the '*bond holder*') to pay a sum of money (the '*capital*') to another (the '*bond issuer*');
- identify assets or a class of assets which the bond issuer will acquire for the purpose of generating income or gains;
- specify a term at the end of which they cease to apply;
- include an undertaking by the bond issuer to dispose of any bond assets still in his possession at the end of the bond term;
- include an undertaking by the bond issuer to make a repayment of the capital to the bond holder during or at the end of the bond term (whether or not in instalments);
- include an undertaking by the bond issuer to make additional payments not exceeding a reasonable commercial return on a loan of the capital during or at the end of the bond term;
- include an undertaking by the bond issuer to arrange for the management of the bond assets with a view to generating sufficient income to pay the redemption payment and the additional payments;
- allow the bond holder to transfer the rights under the arrangements;
- are a listed security on a recognised stock exchange (see **63.28** SHARES AND SECURITIES) in the UK, EEA or Gibraltar or, for 2018/19 onwards (for corporation tax purposes for accounting periods beginning on or after 1 April 2018) admitted to trading on a multilateral trading facility (as defined); and
- are wholly or partly treated in accordance with international accounting standards as a financial liability of the bond issuer (or would be if he applied them).

The '*alternative finance return*' is equal to the additional payments.

[*TCGA 1992, ss 151N, 151S(3); FA 2018, s 34(2)(4); SI 2019 No 689, Regs 1, 6(13); European Union (Withdrawal Agreement) Act 2020, Sch 5 para 1(1)*].

Further consequences for diminishing shared ownership arrangements

[3.3] HMRC have published their view of the chargeable gains consequences arising where a person acquires an asset under a diminishing shared ownership arrangement. In their view, unless there are any special features leading to a different conclusion, the buyer is treated as acquiring each successive tranche of beneficial interest at the time they entered into the unconditional contracts with the seller and the financial institution. Where this is the case it follows that the date of acquisition of the asset for the purposes of indexation allowance (where available) is the date the diminishing shared ownership arrangements were entered into. (HMRC Brief 26/07).

A diminishing shared ownership arrangement is not a partnership for capital gains tax purposes. [*TCGA 1992, s 151Y*].

Further consequences for investment bond arrangements

[3.4] An alternative finance arrangement which is an investment bond arrangement is a security, but is neither an offshore fund nor a unit trust scheme, for capital gains purposes. [*TCGA 1992, ss 151V, 151W*].

Such an arrangement is also a qualifying corporate bond if certain conditions are met — see **54.3** QUALIFYING CORPORATE BONDS.

The bond holder is not treated as having a legal or beneficial interest in the bond assets and the bond issuer is not treated as a trustee of the assets. Gains accruing to the bond issuer in connection with the bond assets are gains of the bond issuer and not of the bond holder. Such gains do not accrue to the bond issuer in a fiduciary or representative capacity. Payments made by the bond issuer are not made in such a capacity. The bond holder is not entitled to relief for capital expenditure incurred in connection with the bond assets. [*TCGA 1992, s 151U*].

Investment bond arrangements where the underlying asset is land

[3.5] The following provisions (together with equivalent provisions relating to stamp duty land tax and capital allowances) are intended to ensure that the tax consequences of an alternative finance investment bond are the same as those for a conventional securitisation of land. The '*effective date*' of a land transaction is that date for the purposes of stamp duty land tax. Where a transaction is to be completed by conveyance, the effective date will in most cases be the date of completion. Where, however, 'substantial performance' of the contract takes place at an earlier date, that earlier date is the effective date. '*Substantial performance*' of a contract occurs when either the purchaser (or connected person) takes possession of substantially the whole of the interest or a substantial amount of the consideration is paid or provided. [*FA 2003, s 44; FA 2009, Sch 61 para 1(2)*]. See Tolley's Stamp Taxes for further details.

Relief for first transaction

Relief applies where:

Alternative Finance Arrangements [3.5]

(a) two persons ('P' and 'Q') enter into arrangements under which P transfers to Q a 'qualifying interest' in land (the '*first transaction*') and P and Q agree that when Q ceases to hold the interest as a 'bond asset' (see (b) below), Q will transfer the interest to P;
(b) Q, as 'bond issuer', enters into an alternative finance investment bond (see **3.2** above), either before or after making the arrangements in (a) above, and holds the interest in land as a bond asset; and
(c) to generate income or gains for the bond, Q and P enter into a leaseback agreement (i.e. Q grants a lease or sub-lease to P out of the interest transferred to Q by the first transaction).

For this purpose, '*bond asset*' and '*bond issuer*' have the same meaning as at **3.2** above. A '*qualifying interest*' in land is a major interest in land (within *FA 2003, s 117*), but leases with a term or period of less than 21 years are excluded. The Treasury can make regulations specifying an alternative to condition (c) above. [*FA 2009, Sch 61 paras 1(1), 5(1)–(5)*].

If all of the above conditions are met within 30 days beginning with the effective date of the first transaction, that transaction is treated for chargeable gains purposes as being neither an acquisition by Q nor a disposal by Q. The granting of the lease or sub-lease under the leaseback agreement in (c) above is treated as neither an acquisition by P nor a disposal by Q. [*FA 2009, Sch 61 para 10*].

Withdrawal of relief

This relief is, however, withdrawn in certain circumstances. For this purpose, the following conditions are relevant.

(i) Within 120 days beginning with the effective date of the first transaction, Q must provide HMRC with evidence prescribed by HMRC in regulations that a satisfactory legal charge has been entered in the register of title kept under *Land Registration Act 2002, s 1* (or Scottish or NI equivalent). For this purpose, a charge is satisfactory if it is a first charge in favour of HMRC over the interest transferred by the first transaction for the amount of stamp duty land tax which would have been chargeable on the first transaction if it had been carried out at market value, together with any interest and penalties.
(ii) The total payments of 'capital' (see **3.2** above) made to Q before the termination of the bond must be not less than 60% of the value of the interest in land at the time of the first transaction.
(iii) (Subject to the substitution of asset rules below) Q must hold the interest in land as a bond asset until the termination of the bond.
(iv) Within 30 days beginning with the date on which the interest in land ceases to be held as a bond asset, it must be transferred by Q back to P (the '*second transaction*').
(v) The second transaction must be effected within ten years after the first transaction (or within a period specified by Treasury regulations).

The relief is withdrawn if:

(A) where the interest is in land in the UK, condition (i) above is not met;
(B) the interest in land is transferred by Q back to P without conditions (ii) and (iii) above having been met;

31

(C) the ten-year period in condition (v) above expires without conditions (ii) and (iii) above having been met; or
(D) it becomes apparent for any other reason at any time that any of conditions (ii) to (v) above cannot or will not be met.

If a chargeable gain or allowable loss arises as a result of the withdrawal of relief, it is treated as accruing:

- where (A) above applies, at the end of the 120-day period;
- where (B) above applies, immediately before the transfer from Q to P;
- where (C) above applies, at the end of the 10-year period; and
- where (D) above applies, at the time it becomes apparent that the conditions cannot or will not be met.

[FA 2009, Sch 61 paras 5(6)–(12), 10, 11].

Relief for second transaction

The second transaction (see (iv) above) is treated for chargeable gains purposes as being neither an acquisition by P nor a disposal by Q if (a) to (c) and (ii) to (v) above are satisfied and, where the land is in the UK, (i) above is satisfied. [FA 2009, Sch 61 para 12].

Substitution of asset

If the interest in land is transferred by Q back to P before the termination of the investment bond (so that condition (iii) above is not met), the above reliefs nevertheless continue to apply if conditions (iv) and (v) above are met and P and Q enter into further arrangements within (a) above relating to another interest in land. The value of the interest in the replacement land at the time it is transferred from P to Q must be equal to or greater than the value of the interest in the original land at the time of the first transaction.

In such circumstances, the reliefs in respect of the original land apply despite the fact that condition (iii) above has not been met, provided that (a)–(c) above and conditions (iii)–(v) above are met in relation to the replacement land.

In relation to the replacement land, condition (ii) above operates by reference to the value or the interest in the original land, and the ten-year limit in (v) above runs from the date of the first transaction relating to the original land.

These provisions also apply, with any necessary modifications where replacement land is itself replaced.

[FA 2009, Sch 61 para 18].

Anti-avoidance

The above reliefs are not available where control of the underlying asset is acquired by a bond holder (see 3.3 above) or a group of connected bond holders. This occurs where the rights of bond holders under a bond include the right of management and control of the bond assets and a bond holder or group acquires sufficient such rights to enable them to exercise that right to the exclusion of any other bond holders.

If the bond holder or group acquire such control before the end of the 30 days beginning with the effective date of the first transaction, no relief is available. If control is acquired at a later date, any relief already given is withdrawn as above.

This provision does not, however, prevent relief being given if either:

- at the time the rights were acquired, the bond holder or holders did not know and had no reason to suspect that the acquisition enabled the exercise of the right of management and control to the exclusion of other bond holders and as soon as reasonably practicable after becoming so aware they transfer sufficient rights for such management and control no longer to be possible; or
- the bond holder underwrites a public offer of rights under the bond and does not exercise the right of management and control of the bond assets.

For this purpose, a person underwrites an offer of rights if he agrees to make payments of capital under the bond in the event that others do not make the payments.

The above reliefs are also not available if the arrangements within (a) above are not made for genuine commercial reasons or form part of arrangements a main purpose of which is the avoidance of liability to income tax, corporation tax, capital gains tax, stamp duty or stamp duty land tax.

[FA 2009, Sch 61 paras 20–22].

4
Anti-Avoidance

Introduction to anti-avoidance	4.1
Approach of the Courts	4.2
General anti-abuse rule	4.3
Procedure	4.4
Protective GAAR notices	4.5
Counteraction of equivalent arrangements	4.6
Application of the GAAR to partnerships	4.7
Specific legislation	4.8
Value shifting	4.9
Value shifting to give tax-free benefit	4.11
Certain disposals of shares by companies	4.12
Connected persons	4.13
Assets disposed of in a series of transactions	4.14
Close company transferring asset at undervalue	4.15
Restrictions on company reconstructions	4.16
Schemes involving the transfer of a business owned by companies	4.17
Depreciatory transactions within groups of companies	4.18
Dividend stripping	4.19
Abuse of concessions	4.20
Factoring of income receipts	4.21
Transfer of income stream	4.22
Disposal of income stream through partnership	4.23
Disposal of asset through partnership	4.24
Follower notices	4.25
Giving of follower notices	4.26
Action required following giving of follower notice	4.27
Late appeal against a judicial ruling	4.28
Accelerated payment notices	4.29
Giving of accelerated payment notice	4.30
Effects of accelerated payment notice	4.31
Serial avoiders regime	4.32
Warning notices	4.33
Meaning of 'relevant defeat'	4.34
Requirement of annual information notices	4.35
Restriction of reliefs	4.36
Partnerships	4.37
Groups of companies	4.38
Penalties	4.39
Publishing taxpayer's details	4.40
Key points on anti-avoidance	4.41

Cross-references. See **15.6** COMPANIES for provisions relating to corporate losses; **18** CONNECTED PERSONS; **21** DISCLOSURE OF TAX AVOIDANCE SCHEMES; **22.9** DOUBLE TAX RELIEF for schemes and arrangements designed to increase such relief; **49**

[4.1] Anti-Avoidance

OVERSEAS MATTERS for provisions relating to overseas resident settlements; **49.9** OVERSEAS MATTERS for interests in controlled foreign companies and in offshore funds respectively; **50.16** PARTNERSHIPS; **62.16** SETTLEMENTS for restrictions on transfer of settlement losses to beneficiary becoming absolutely entitled to settled property; **62.20–62.23** SETTLEMENTS for further anti-avoidance provisions.

Introduction to anti-avoidance

[4.1] Anyone attempting to structure a transaction so as to avoid a liability to tax on chargeable gains arising or to mitigate such a liability must consider:

(a) whether the line of cases often referred to as the 'Ramsay principle' will operate to make the arrangements ineffective;
(b) whether the tax advantage under the arrangements is counteracted by the general anti-abuse rule;
(c) whether the arrangements give rise to a duty to disclose the details to HMRC under the provisions for DISCLOSURE OF TAX AVOIDANCE SCHEMES (**21**); and
(d) whether the arrangements fall foul of one of the many pieces of specific anti-avoidance legislation.

This chapter covers three of these considerations. For (c) above see **21** DISCLOSURE OF TAX AVOIDANCE SCHEMES.

The approach of the courts to avoidance cases is dealt with at **4.2** below, and the rules for the disclosure of tax avoidance schemes are at **21.2–21.5**. The general anti-abuse rule is described at **4.3–4.7** below. The next part of the chapter describes specific anti-avoidance provisions, many of which, it should be noted, apply where the particular conditions are satisfied whether or not there is any intention to avoid tax. Note that there are many anti-avoidance provisions which are dealt with outside this chapter where they relate to legislation described elsewhere in this work. See the list of provisions at **4.8** below and the cross references at the head of the chapter.

HMRC have powers, by way of a 'follower notice' to require a person using an avoidance scheme which is defeated in the courts in relation to another taxpayer to concede their position to reflect the court's decision. See **4.25** onwards below. Powers to enable HMRC to issue an 'accelerated payment notice' which requires a user of an avoidance scheme to pay tax upfront before the success or failure of the scheme has been finally determined have also been introduced. See **4.29** onwards below.

There is a regime of warnings and escalating sanctions for taxpayers ('serial avoiders') who persistently engage in tax avoidance schemes that are defeated by HMRC. See **4.32–4.40** below.

In March 2020, HMRC published a new approach to tackling promoters of mass-marketed avoidance schemes. See www.gov.uk/government/publications/tackling-promoters-of-mass-marketed-tax-avoidance-schemes/tackling-promoters-of-mass-marketed-tax-avoidance-schemes.

Approach of the Courts

[4.2] For the general approach of the Courts to transactions entered into solely to avoid or reduce tax liability, leading cases are *Duke of Westminster v CIR* HL 1935, 19 TC 490; *W T Ramsay Ltd v CIR; Eilbeck v Rawling* HL 1981, 54 TC 101; *CIR v Burmah Oil Co Ltd* HL 1981, 54 TC 200; *Furniss v Dawson (and related appeals)* HL 1984, 55 TC 324. See also *Coates v Arndale Properties Ltd* HL 1984, 59 TC 516; *Reed v Nova Securities Ltd* HL 1985, 59 TC 516; *Magnavox Electronics Co Ltd (in liquidation) v Hall* CA 1986, 59 TC 610; *Commissioner of Inland Revenue v Challenge Corporation Ltd* PC, [1986] STC 548; *Craven v White; CIR v Bowater Property Developments Ltd; Baylis v Gregory* HL 1988, 62 TC 1; *Dunstan v Young Austen Young Ltd* CA 1988, 61 TC 448; *Shepherd v Lyntress Ltd; News International plc v Shepherd* Ch D 1989, 62 TC 495; *Ensign Tankers (Leasing) Ltd v Stokes* HL 1992, 64 TC 617; *Moodie v CIR and another (and related appeals)* HL 1993, 65 TC 610; *Countess Fitzwilliam and others v CIR (and related appeals)* HL 1993, 67 TC 614; *Pigott v Staines Investments Co Ltd* Ch D 1995, 68 TC 342; *CIR v McGuckian* HL 1997, 69 TC 1; *MacNiven v Westmoreland Investments Ltd* HL 2001, 73 TC 1; *CIR v Scottish Provident Institution* HL 2004, [2005] STC 15; *Mawson v Barclays Mercantile Business Finance Ltd* HL 2004, [2005] STC 1 and *HMRC v Tower Mcashback LLP1* SC, [2011] UKSC 19.

See also *DR Collins v HMRC* (Sp C 675), [2008] SSCD 718, *Trustees of the Eyretel Unapproved Pension Scheme v HMRC*, (Sp C 718), [2009] SSCD 17, *Mayes v HMRC* CA [2011] EWCA Civ 407; 2011 STI 1444, *Berry v HMRC* UT, [2011] STC 1057 and *Explainaway Ltd v HMRC* UT, [2012] STC 2525.

Classical interpretation

The classical interpretation of the constraints upon the courts in deciding cases involving tax avoidance schemes is summed up in Lord Tomlin's statement in the *Duke of Westminster* case that 'every man is entitled if he can to order his affairs so that the tax attaching . . . is less than it otherwise would be'. The judgment was concerned with the tax consequences of a single transaction, but in *Ramsay*, and subsequently in *Furniss v Dawson*, the House of Lords has set bounds on the ambit within which this principle can be applied in relation to modern sophisticated and increasingly artificial arrangements to avoid tax. In *CIR v McGuckian*, it was observed that while Lord Tomlin's words in the *Duke of Westminster* case 'still point to a material consideration, namely the general liberty of the citizen to arrange his financial affairs as he thinks fit, they have ceased to be canonical as to the tax consequences of a tax avoidance scheme'. It was further observed that the *Ramsay* approach was 'more natural and less extreme' than the majority decision in *Duke of Westminster*.

The 'Ramsay' approach

Ramsay concerned a complex 'circular' avoidance scheme at the end of which the financial position of the parties was little changed but it was claimed that a large capital gains tax loss had been created. It was held that where a preconceived series of transactions is entered into to avoid tax and with the clear intention to proceed through all stages to completion, once set in motion, the Duke of Westminster principle does not compel a consideration of the individual transactions and of the fiscal consequences of such transactions in isolation. The opinions of the House of Lords in *Furniss v Dawson* are of outstanding importance, and establish, *inter alia*, that the *Ramsay* principle is not confined to 'circular' devices, and that if a series of transactions is 'preordained', a particular transaction within the series, accepted as genuine, may nevertheless be ignored if it was entered into solely for fiscal reasons and without any commercial purpose other than tax avoidance, even if the series of transactions as a whole has a legitimate commercial purpose.

However, in *Craven v White* the House of Lords indicated that for the *Ramsay* principle to apply all the transactions in a series have to be preordained with such a degree of certainty that, at the time of the earlier transactions, there is no practical likelihood that the transactions would not take place. It is not sufficient that the ultimate transaction is simply of a kind that was envisaged at the time of the earlier transactions. See, however, *CIR v Scottish Provident Institution* below. In the unanimous decision of the House of Lords in *Ensign Tankers (Leasing) Ltd v Stokes*, the lead judgment drew a clear distinction between 'tax avoidance' and 'tax mitigation', it being said that the *Duke of Westminster* principle is accurate as far as the latter is concerned but does not apply to the former.

Fitzwilliam involved five transactions entered into over a short period of time to avoid capital transfer tax on appointments from a will trust, the last four transactions being determined by the Revenue to form a preordained series of transactions subject to the *Ramsay* principle but which the taxpayers claimed should be viewed separately with the result that by reason of a number of available reliefs no liability to capital transfer tax arose. The House of Lords stated that the correct approach to a consideration of steps 2 to 5 was to ask whether realistically they constituted a single and indivisible whole in which one or more of the steps was simply an element without independent effect and whether it was intellectually possible so to treat them. It was held that both questions should be answered in the negative. The case put by the Revenue did not depend on disregarding for fiscal purposes any one or more of steps 2 to 5 as having been introduced for fiscal purposes only and as having no independent effect, nor on treating the whole of steps 2 to 5 as having no such effect. Each of the four steps had a fiscal effect of giving rise to an income tax charge on two of the taxpayers for a period of time, and there was a potential capital transfer tax charge should either have died whilst in enjoyment of the income associated with the transactions. Although steps 2 to 5 were 'preordained', in the sense that they formed part of a pre-planned tax avoidance scheme and that there was no reasonable possibility that they would not all be carried out, the fact of preordainment in that sense was not sufficient in itself to negative the application of an exemption from liability to tax which the series of transactions was intended to create, unless the series was capable of being construed in a manner inconsistent with the application of the exemption. In the particular circumstances of the case, the series of transactions could not be so construed. Two or more transactions in the series could not be run together, as in *Furniss v Dawson*, nor could any one or more of them be disregarded. There was no rational basis on which the four separate steps could be treated as effective for the purposes of one provision which created a charge to tax on a termination of an interest in possession but ineffective for the purposes of two other provisions which gave exemptions from that charge where the interest was disposed of for a consideration and where the interest reverted to the settlor. Accordingly, the case was one to which the *Ramsay* principle, as extended by *Furniss v Dawson*, did not apply.

In *MacNiven v Westmoreland Investments Ltd*, where the HL held that the *Ramsay* principle did not apply to a payment of interest, Lord Nicholls held that 'the very phrase "the *Ramsay* principle" is potentially misleading. In *Ramsay* the House did not enunciate any new legal principle. What the House did was to highlight that, confronted with new and sophisticated tax avoidance devices, the courts' duty is to determine the legal nature of the transactions in question and then relate them to the fiscal legislation'. Lord Hoffmann held that 'what Lord Wilberforce was doing in the *Ramsay* case was no more . . . than to treat the statutory words "loss" and "disposal" as referring to commercial concepts to which a juristic analysis of the transaction, treating each step as autonomous and independent, might not be determinative'. Lord Hutton held that 'an essential element of a transaction to which the *Ramsay* principle is applicable is that it should be artificial'.

In *Mawson v Barclays Mercantile Business Finance Ltd* the HL held that Lord Hoffman's distinction in *Westmoreland* between 'legal' and 'commercial' concepts was not 'intended to provide a substitute for a close analysis of what the statute means'. It 'does not justify the assumption that an answer can be obtained by classifying all concepts a priori as either "commercial" or "legal"'. Instead, in applying any statutory provision, it is necessary 'first, to decide, on a purposive construction, exactly what transaction will answer to the statutory description and secondly, whether the transaction in question does so'.

In *CIR v Scottish Provident Institution* the issue was whether the decision in *Craven v White* meant that a series of transactions could not be treated as a composite transaction under the *Ramsay* principle because there was a real commercial risk that the transactions would not take place. The HL held that 'it would destroy the value of the *Ramsay* principle . . . as referring to the effect of composite transactions if their composite effect had to be disregarded simply because the parties had deliberately included a commercially irrelevant contingency, creating an acceptable risk that the scheme might not work as planned'. Such a 'commercially irrelevant contingency' was found to be present in a purchased tax scheme involving options in *Schofield v HMRC* CA, [2012] STC 2019.

See also *Exors of Connell v HMRC* FTT, [2016] UKFTT 154 (TC); 2016 STI 1802 (market value of loan notes) and *Trustees of the Morrison 2002 Maintenance Trust v HMRC* CA, [2019] STC 400 (disposal of shares by trustees involving intermediate sale to non-resident trust).

Sham

In *Hitch and Others v Stone* CA, [2001] STC 214, the Revenue mounted a successful challenge to a complex and artificial tax avoidance scheme on the grounds that agreements on which it was based were shams. It was noted that 'sham' meant acts done or documents executed by the parties thereto which were intended by them to give to third parties or to the court the appearance of creating between the parties legal rights and obligations different from the actual legal rights and obligations (if any) which the parties intended to create. The law did not require that in every situation every party to the act or document should be a party to the sham, although a case where a document was properly held to be only in part a sham would be the exception rather than the rule and would occur only where the document reflected a transaction divisible into several parts.

Simon's Taxes. See A2.115–A2.123.

General anti-abuse rule

[4.3] The general anti-abuse rule ('GAAR') is intended to counteract the 'tax advantages' arising from 'tax arrangements' which are 'abusive'. Adjustments under the GAAR do not generally take effect until HMRC have referred the case to an independent GAAR Advisory Panel established by the Commissioners for HMRC. Before 22 July 2020, HMRC were generally required to refer the case to the Panel before making an adjustment, subject to the right to make a provisional counteraction before referral to the Panel where, for example, assessing time limits were about to expire. With effect from 22 July 2020, provisional counteraction is replaced with a system of protective GAAR notices. A GAAR Advisory Panel opinion allows HMRC to apply the GAAR to equivalent arrangements used by other taxpayers without further referral.

The GAAR applies to a range of taxes including income tax, corporation tax and capital gains tax.

[FA 2013, s 206].

HMRC do not give formal or informal clearances that the GAAR does not apply. As part of their engagement with large businesses and wealthy individuals, however, HMRC do discuss commercial arrangements and confirm where appropriate that they don't regard particular arrangements as tax avoidance. See www.gov.uk/government/collections/seeking-clearance-or-approval-for-a-transaction.

The GAAR Advisory Panel's published opinion notices are available at www.gov.uk/government/collections/tax-avoidance-general-anti-abuse-rule-gaar.

Definitions

Arrangements are '*tax arrangements*' if, having regard to all the circumstances, it would be reasonable to conclude that the obtaining of a tax advantage was the main purpose, or one of the main purposes, of the arrangements. For this purpose, '*arrangements*' include any agreement, understanding, scheme, transaction or series of transactions, whether or not legally enforceable.

Tax arrangements are '*abusive*' if entering into them or carrying them out cannot reasonably be regarded as a reasonable course of action in relation to the relevant tax provisions, having regard to all the circumstances. Those circumstances include:

- whether the substantive results of the arrangements are consistent with any express or implied principles on which the provisions are based and their policy objectives;

- whether the means of achieving the results of the arrangements involve one or more contrived or abnormal steps; and
- whether the arrangements are intended to exploit any shortcomings in the provisions.

Where the tax arrangements form part of other arrangements, regard must be had to those other arrangements.

The legislation gives the following non-exhaustive examples of what might indicate that tax arrangements are abusive.

- The arrangements result in taxable income, profits or gains significantly less than the economic amount.
- The arrangements result in a tax deduction or loss significantly greater than the economic amount.
- The arrangements result in a claim for repayment or crediting of tax, including foreign tax, that has not been, and is unlikely to be, paid.

The legislation also gives an example of what might indicate that arrangements are not abusive: the arrangements accord with established practice accepted by HMRC.

A *'tax advantage'* includes relief or increased relief from tax, repayment or increased repayment of tax, avoidance or reduction of a charge or assessment to tax, avoidance of a possible assessment to tax or of an obligation to deduct or account for tax, deferral of a payment of tax, and advancement of a repayment of tax.

[FA 2013, ss 207, 208, 214(1)].

Effect of the GAAR

The GAAR operates by counteracting the tax advantage under the tax arrangements by the making of adjustments that are just and reasonable, whether by HMRC or anyone else (the taxpayer or a responsible partner — see **4.7** below). Adjustments can be made by assessment, modification of an assessment, amendment or disallowance of a claim or otherwise. An adjustment can impose a tax liability where there would not otherwise be one or can increase an existing liability. Adjustments may be made in respect of the tax in question or any other tax to which the GAAR applies. Adjustments have effect for all tax purposes. The normal time limits for making assessments etc apply to the making of GAAR adjustments.

The effects of an adjustment under the GAAR are normally suspended until HMRC have followed the appropriate procedures at **4.4**, **4.6** or **4.7** below. Before 22 July 2020, HMRC had to follow the appropriate procedures *before* making an adjustment under the GAAR, subject, with effect from 15 September 2016, to the right to make a provisional counteraction before referral to the Panel where, for example, assessing time limits were about to expire (see **4.5** below). With effect from 22 July 2020, provisional counteraction is replaced with a system of protective GAAR notices (see **4.5** below).

Where a matter is referred to the GAAR Advisory Panel (see **4.4**(4) or (6) and **4.7**(5) and (7) below), adjustments to counteract the tax advantage cannot be made in the *'closed period'* beginning with the 31st day after the end of the

45-day period for making representations (see **4.4**(2) and **4.7**(2) below) and ending immediately before the day on which notice is given of HMRC's final decision after considering the opinion of the Panel. Similarly, adjustments cannot be made in the closed period following the issue of a pooling notice or notice of binding (see **4.6**, **4.7** below). For this purpose, the 'closed period' is defined at **4.6** below.

[*FA 2013, s 209; FA 2020, Sch 14 paras 2, 10, 15; FA 2021, Sch 32 para 3*].

Consequential adjustments

Where the counteraction of a tax advantage is final and, if the counteraction was not made as a result of an HMRC final counteraction notice, the taxpayer or responsible partner (see **4.7** below) has notified HMRC of it, a person (not necessarily the taxpayer or responsible partner) has 12 months, beginning with the day the counteraction becomes final, to make a claim for one or more consequential adjustments to be made in respect of any tax to which the GAAR applies. For this purpose, counteraction of a tax advantage is final when the adjustments made and any amounts resulting from them can no longer be varied, on appeal or otherwise.

Consequential adjustments can be made for any period and may affect any person, whether or not a party to the tax arrangements. Adjustments are made on a just and reasonable basis but cannot increase a person's liability to any tax. HMRC must notify the person who made the claim of any adjustments made in writing. Consequential adjustments can be made by assessment, modification of an assessment, amendment of a claim or otherwise. There are no time limits for making such an adjustment.

The procedure for claims made outside a return in *TMA 1970, Sch 1A* (see **14.3** CLAIMS) applies to claims for consequential adjustments for income tax, capital gains tax and corporation tax purposes. See *FA 2013, s 210(6)* for the procedure rules for other taxes.

[*FA 2013, s 210; FA 2021, Sch 32 para 6*].

See **52.14** PENALTIES for the 60% penalty which applies to arrangements which are counteracted by the GAAR.

Court and tribunal proceedings

In any court or tribunal proceedings in connection with the GAAR, HMRC must show both that the tax arrangements are abusive and that the adjustments made to counteract the tax advantage are just and reasonable.

In making a decision in connection with the GAAR a court or tribunal must take into account any HMRC guidance on the GAAR which was approved by the GAAR Advisory Panel at the time the tax arrangements were entered into and also any relevant opinion of the sub-panel (see **4.4**(9) and **4.6** below).

[*FA 2013, s 211*].

Priority rules

The GAAR can override any priority rule in tax legislation, i.e. any rule to the effect that particular provisions have effect to the exclusion of, or otherwise in priority to, anything else. [*FA 2013, s 212*].

Procedure under the GAAR

[4.4] The normal procedure which HMRC must follow under the GAAR is set out below. See **4.5** below for alternative procedures where a protective GAAR notice is issued or, before 22 July 2020, a provisional counteraction notice was issued. See **4.6** below for alternative procedures in respect of equivalent arrangements. See **4.7** below for the modified normal procedure which applies with effect from 10 June 2021 to counteract tax advantages included in partnership returns.

(1)   An HMRC officer designated by the Commissioners for HMRC for the purpose of the GAAR must give the taxpayer a written notice specifying:
- the arrangements and the tax advantage;
- why the officer considers that a tax advantage has arisen from abusive tax arrangements;
- the counteraction which the officer considers should be taken;
- the period within which the taxpayer can make representations (see (2) below); and
- the effect of the rules in (3)–(5) below and of the PENALTIES (**52.14**) which may apply if the proposed counteraction takes effect.

The notice may set out steps that the taxpayer may take to avoid the application of the GAAR.

Where a notice is given on or after 22 July 2020, the adjustments specified in it have effect as if they were made under *FA 2013, s 209* (see **4.3** above under 'Effects of the GAAR'). This rule does not apply if a protective GAAR notice or a provisional counteraction notice have already been given in respect of the specified adjustments (see **4.5** below). The notice must normally be given within the normal time limits for assessments applicable to the proposed adjustments, but if the taxpayer's return is under enquiry and the adjustments relate to matters included in the return, the notice can be given at any time until the time the enquiry is completed.

If no appeal is made in respect of the adjustments or an appeal is withdrawn or determined by agreement, and no final counteraction notice is given under (10) below or the provisions at **4.6** below, the notice has effect as if it was a final counteraction notice (and therefore, as if the procedural requirements had been met). A penalty under *FA 2013, s 212A* (see **52.14** PENALTIES) cannot, however, be charged. In any other case, the specified adjustments have no effect unless they (or lesser adjustments) are subsequently specified in a final counteraction notice. The time limits for making the final counteraction notice are treated as met by the giving of the original notice.

(2)   The taxpayer has 45 days starting with the day on which HMRC's notice is given to send written representations in response to the notice to the designated HMRC officer. The designated officer may extend the period if the taxpayer makes a written request.

(3)   Where a person who has been given a notice under (1) takes 'corrective action' before the beginning of the closed period (see **4.3** above under 'Effect of the GAAR'), the matter is not referred to the GAAR Advisory Panel under (4) or (6) below. A person takes '*corrective action*' for this purpose only if he amends a return or claim to counteract the tax

advantage or relinquishes the tax advantage by entering into a written agreement with HMRC to do so. A person can amend a return or claim for this purpose during an enquiry even if the normal time limits have expired. No appeal may then be made against any enquiry closure notice (see **58.13** RETURNS) to the extent that it takes into account an amendment made as corrective action. The person must notify HMRC of the action taken and the additional tax amount which has or will become due. Where a person takes corrective action in this way no penalty can be charged under the provisions at **52.14** PENALTIES.

(4) If the taxpayer makes no representations and, where relevant, does not take corrective action, a designated HMRC officer must refer the matter to the GAAR Advisory Panel.

The officer must at the same time notify the taxpayer that the matter is being referred. The notice must inform the taxpayer of the period for making representations under (7) below and of the requirement to send any such representations to the officer. The officer must provide the Panel with a copy of the notice given to the taxpayer at step (1) above and the notice informing the taxpayer that the matter has been referred to the Panel.

(5) If the taxpayer does make representations but, where relevant, does not take corrective action, the representations must be considered by a designated HMRC officer.

(6) If the designated HMRC officer in (5) above still considers that the GAAR should apply, he must refer the matter to the GAAR Advisory Panel, together with a copy of the taxpayer's representations and any comments he has on those representations. The officer must notify the taxpayer of his decision on whether or not to refer the matter to the GAAR Advisory Panel as soon as is reasonably practicable.

The same requirements for the officer to notify the taxpayer and to provide information to the Panel apply as at step (4) above. The notice to the taxpayer must, however, also include a copy of any comments on the taxpayer's representations sent by the officer to the Panel.

(7) The taxpayer has 21 days to send written representations to the Panel and the designated HMRC officer about the notice given at step (1) above and any comments made by HMRC on the taxpayer's original representations. The Panel may extend the period for making representations if the taxpayer makes a written request.

(8) If the taxpayer makes representations at step (7) above but did not make representations at step (2) above, the designated HMRC officer may provide the Panel and the taxpayer with comments on the step (7) representations.

(9) A sub-panel of three members of the Panel will consider the matter in question. The sub-panel may invite the taxpayer or the designated HMRC officer to supply further information within a specified period. Information supplied to the sub-panel must also be sent to the other party.

The sub-panel must produce an opinion notice stating its collective opinion as to whether or not the entering into and carrying out of the tax arrangements was a reasonable course of action in relation to the relevant tax provisions, having regard to the circumstances outlined at

Where a notice within (2)–(4) above specifies lesser adjustments, the provisional counteraction notice must be amended accordingly (unless it was issued after the notice in (2)–(4) above).

If a notice within (2) above is given and the matter is not referred to the GAAR Advisory Panel or if a notice within (2)–(4) above is given and subsequently the taxpayer is given a notice stating that the tax advantage is not to be counteracted under the GAAR, the adjustments in the provisional counteraction notice are treated as cancelled unless HMRC have the power to make the adjustments under provisions other than the GAAR and they state that the adjustments are therefore not cancelled. If a notice within (4) above is withdrawn, the adjustments in the provisional counteraction notice are likewise treated as cancelled, subject to the same exception.

Where a notice within (2)–(4) above is given and subsequently the taxpayer is given a notice stating that the tax advantage is to be counteracted, the adjustments in the provisional counteraction notice are confirmed so far as specified in the notice as adjustments required to give effect to the counteraction and are otherwise treated as cancelled.

[FA 2013, ss 209A–209F; FA 2020, Sch 14 paras 6, 13, 15].

Counteraction of equivalent arrangements

[4.6] There are provisions to enable the counteraction of 'equivalent' arrangements entered into by other taxpayers. The provisions enable HMRC to issue a 'pooling notice'

A designated HMRC officer may issue a *'pooling notice'* to a taxpayer (R), where:

(a) a person (P) has been given a notice under **4.4**(1) above or **4.7**(1) below in relation to tax arrangements (*'lead arrangements'*);
(b) the 45-day period for representations in **4.4**(2) above or **4.7**(2) below has expired but no final counteraction notice under **4.4**(10) above, **4.7**(11) below or the generic referral provisions below has been given in respect of the matter;
(c) the officer considers that a tax advantage has arisen, or may have arisen, to R from tax arrangements which are abusive;
(d) the officer considers that those arrangements are equivalent to the lead arrangements; and
(e) the officer considers that the advantage should be counteracted.

The notice places R's arrangements in a pool comprising all the arrangements in relation to which pooling notices have been served in respect of the lead arrangements (whether under these provisions or those for partnerships at **4.7** below). Before 5 December 2017, the lead arrangements were themselves in the pool along with the equivalent arrangements. A pooling notice may not be given if R has already been given a notice under **4.4**(1) above.

A designated HMRC officer may issue a *'notice of binding'* to a taxpayer (R), where:

(i) a person has been given a final counteraction notice under **4.4**(10) above, **4.7**(11) below or the generic referral provisions below in relation to tax arrangements (*'counteracted arrangements'*) which are in a pool;

[4.6] Anti-Avoidance

(ii) the officer considers that a tax advantage has arisen, or may have arisen, to R from tax arrangements which are abusive;
(iii) the officer considers that those arrangements are equivalent to the counteracted arrangements; and
(iv) the officer considers that the advantage should be counteracted.

A notice of binding may not be given if R has already been given a pooling notice or a notice under **4.4**(1) above or **4.7**(1) below.

A pooling notice or notice of binding must be given as soon as is reasonably practicable after HMRC become aware of the relevant facts. The notice must specify the tax arrangements and tax advantage concerned; explain why the officer considers them to be equivalent to the lead arrangements or the counteracted arrangements and why a tax advantage is considered to have arisen from abusive arrangements; set out the counteraction that the officer considers should be taken; and the effects of the notice. It may, but is not required to, set out steps which can be taken to avoid the proposed counteraction.

Where a pooling notice or notice of binding is given on or after 22 July 2020, the adjustments specified in it have effect as if they were made under *FA 2013, s 209* (see **4.3** above under 'Effects of the GAAR'). This rule does not apply if a protective GAAR notice or a provisional counteraction notice have already been given in respect of the specified adjustments (see **4.5** below). The notice must normally be given within the normal time limits for assessments applicable to the proposed adjustments but if the taxpayer's return is under enquiry and the adjustments relate to matters included in the return, the notice can be given at any time until the time the enquiry is completed.

If no appeal is made in respect of the adjustments or an appeal is withdrawn or determined by agreement, and no final counteraction notice (see below, **4.4**(10) above and **4.7**(11) below) is given, the notice has effect as if it were a final counteraction notice (and therefore as if the procedural requirements had been met). A penalty under *FA 2013, s 212A or s 212B* (see **52.14** PENALTIES) cannot, however, be charged. In any other case, the specified adjustments have no effect unless they (or lesser adjustments) are subsequently specified in a final counteraction notice. The time limits for making the final counteraction notice are treated as met by the giving of the pooling notice or notice of binding.

Arrangements are '*equivalent*' if they are substantially the same as one another, having regard to their results, the means of achieving those results, and the characteristics on the basis of which it could reasonably be argued in each case that the arrangements are abusive tax arrangements under which a tax advantage has arisen.

Where a person who has been given a pooling notice or a notice of binding takes 'corrective action' before the beginning of the 'closed period', he is treated as not having been given the notice and the arrangements are accordingly no longer in the pool. A person takes '*corrective action*' for this purpose only if he amends a return or claim to counteract the tax advantage or relinquishes the tax advantage by entering into an agreement with HMRC to determine an appeal. A person can amend a return or claim for this purpose during an enquiry even if the normal time limits have expired. No appeal may then be made against any enquiry closure notice (see **58.13** RETURNS) to the extent that it takes into account an amendment made as corrective action. The person must notify HMRC of the action taken and the additional tax amount which has or will become due. The '*closed period*' begins on the 31st day after the day on which the pooling notice or notice of binding was given. In the case of a pooling notice, the closed period ends immediately before the day on which notice is given of HMRC's final decision after considering the opinion of the GAAR Advisory Panel (see below). In the case of a notice of binding, the period is treated as ending at the same time as it begins. Where a person takes corrective action in this way, no penalty can be charged under the provisions at **52.14** PENALTIES.

Before 5 December 2017, if P in (a) above takes corrective action within the 75-day period beginning with the day on which the notice under **4.4**(1) above was given, the lead arrangements are treated as ceasing to be in the pool. (On and after that date, the lead arrangements are not pooled in any case.)

Where, after a pooling notice has been issued to a person, the GAAR Advisory Panel issue an opinion notice (see **4.4**(9) above) in respect of another set of arrangements in the pool (the '*referred arrangements*'), the HMRC officer must give the person a '*pooled arrangements opinion notice*' setting out a report of the opinion and the person's right to make representations. Only one such notice may be given to a person about the same arrangements. The taxpayer has 30 days from the date of the notice to make representations that no tax advantage has arisen or that his arrangements are materially different from the referred arrangements.

The HMRC officer must consider any opinion of the GAAR Advisory Panel about the referred arrangements, together with any representations made, and issue a written notice with his decision as to whether the tax arrangements under consideration are to be counteracted under the GAAR. If so, the notice must set out the adjustments required to give effect to the counteraction and any steps that the taxpayer must take to give effect to it.

Where an HMRC officer gives a notice of binding, he must at the same time give a '*bound arrangements opinion notice*' setting out a report of any opinion of the GAAR Advisory Panel about the counteracted arrangements and the person's right to make representations. The taxpayer has 30 days from the date of the notice to make representations that no tax advantage has arisen to him or that his arrangements are materially different from the counteracted arrangements.

The HMRC officer must then consider any opinion of the GAAR Advisory Panel about the counteracted arrangements, together with any representations made, and issue a written notice (a final counteraction notice) with his decision as to whether the tax arrangements under consideration are to counteracted under the GAAR. If so, the notice must set out the adjustments required to give effect to the counteraction and any steps that the taxpayer must take to give effect to it.

See **4.7** below for modifications to these provisions which apply with effect from 10 June 2021 to counteract tax advantages included in partnership returns.

[4.6] Anti-Avoidance

[FA 2013, ss 209(9), 209AB, 209ABA, 209AC, Schs 43A, 43D para 12; FA 2020, Sch 14 paras 4, 8, 12, 15; FA 2021, Sch 32 paras 1, 3(4), 4, 5, 11; SI 2017 No 1090, Regs 1–10].

Generic referral of equivalent arrangements to the GAAR Advisory Panel

There are provisions for HMRC to make a generic referral to the GAAR Advisory Panel of arrangements in a pool.

Where:

(A) (on or after 5 December 2017) further to pooling notices given as above, two or more sets of arrangements are in a pool relating to any lead arrangements, and P in (a) above took corrective action within the 75-day period beginning with the day on which the notice under **4.4**(1) was given (or within such longer period as P and HMRC may have agreed); or

(B) (before 5 December 2017) pooling notices had placed one or more sets of arrangements in a pool with lead arrangements, and those lead arrangements ceased to be in the pool,

then, provided none of the pooled arrangements have been referred to the GAAR Advisory Panel (see **4.4**(4), (6) above and **4.7**(5) and (7) below) a designated HMRC officer may give to each of the taxpayers whose arrangements are in the pool a notice of a proposal to make a generic referral to the Panel in respect of the arrangements in the pool. The notices must specify the arrangements and the tax advantage and the period within which the taxpayer can make a proposal (see below).

A person who has been given a notice has 30 days beginning with the day the notice was given to propose to HMRC that they should give him a notice under **4.4**(1) above or **4.7**(1) below and should not proceed with the generic referral.

If none of the notified taxpayers makes such a proposal within the 30-day period, the HMRC officer must make a referral (a '*generic referral*') to the GAAR Advisory Panel. If at least one of the recipients makes a proposal within the 30-day period, the officer must, after that period ends, decide whether to give one of the taxpayers a notice under **4.4**(1) above or **4.7**(1) below or to make a generic referral. On and after 5 December 2017, the officer must make a generic referral if a taxpayer is duly given a notice under **4.4**(1) above or **4.7**(1) below but the matter is not referred to the GAAR Advisory Panel.

Where HMRC make a generic referral to the GAAR Advisory Panel, the designated HMRC officer must provide the Panel with a general statement of the material characteristics of the arrangements together with a declaration that this is applicable to *all* the arrangements and that nothing material to the panel's consideration has been omitted. The general statement must contain a factual description as well as HMRC's opinion, and a copy must be provided to the taxpayers.

A sub-panel of three members of the Panel will consider the referral. The sub-panel must produce an opinion notice stating its collective opinion as to whether or not the entering into and carrying out of the tax arrangements described in the general statement was a reasonable course of action in relation to the relevant tax provisions. An opinion notice may indicate that the sub-panel considers that it is not possible to reach a view on the information available. Alternatively, the sub-panel may produce two or three opinion notices which, taken together, state the opinions of all the members. An opinion notice must include the reasons for the opinion and is given to the designated HMRC officer.

The HMRC officer must then provide a copy of the opinion notice (or notices) to each taxpayer, any one of whom may then, within 30 days, make representations that:

- no tax advantage has arisen to him;
- he has already been given a bound arrangements opinion notice in relation to the arrangements concerned (see above); or
- a matter set out in HMRC's general statement is materially incorrect.

The officer must then, for each taxpayer, consider any opinion of the GAAR Advisory Panel, together with any representations made, and send a written notice (a final counteraction notice) with his decision as to whether the tax arrangements under consideration are to counteracted under the GAAR. If so, the notice must set out the adjustments required to give effect to the counter-action and the steps that the taxpayer must take to give effect to it.

[FA 2013, s 214(3), Sch 43B; FA 2021, Sch 32 para 12; SI 2017 No 1090, Regs 1, 11–14].

Application of the GAAR to partnerships

[4.7] *Finance Act 2021* introduced provisions intended to enable the GAAR procedures to operate in the same way as that in which HMRC conduct enquiries into partnerships, allowing, for example, notices to be given via the representative partner, making amendments to the partnership return and feeding counteraction through to each partners' tax returns. The provisions apply with effect from 10 June 2021, regardless of when the tax arrangements were entered into and apply where a partnership return has been made under *TMA 1970, s 12AA* (see **58.17** RETURNS). They will also apply where a partnership return is made under the making tax digital provisions of *TMA 1970, Sch A1 para 10*. [*FA 2013, Sch 43D para 1; FA 2021, s 124, Sch 32 para 1*].

For the purposes of the provisions, the *'responsible partner'* is the person who delivered the partnership return or their successor (see **58.17** RETURNS for the appointment of a successor where a partner responsible for dealing with a return ceases to be available) or, in the case of a return under *TMA 1970, Sch A1*, the nominated partner. A partnership return is treated as made on the basis that a particular tax advantage arises to a partner from particular arrangements if it is made on the basis that an increase or decrease in any amounts included in the partnership statement (see **58.18** RETURNS) result from the arrangements and that increase or decrease results in a tax advantage for the partner. [*FA 2013, Sch 43D paras 2, 3; FA 2021, Sch 32 para 1*].

[4.7] Anti-Avoidance

Protective GAAR notice

An HMRC officer may issue a protective GAAR notice to the responsible partner, stating that a return was made on the basis that a tax advantage might have arisen to one or more partners from abusive tax arrangements and that, if so, it ought to be counteracted under the GAAR. Where such a notice is given, the provisions relating to protective GAAR notices at **4.5** above apply, with necessary modifications. In particular, where the notice has effect as if it were a final counteraction notice, a penalty under *FA 2013, s 212B* (see **52.14** PENALTIES) cannot be charged. [*FA 2013, Sch 43D para 4; FA 2021, Sch 32 para 1*].

Modification of normal procedure

The provisions apply the normal GAAR procedure outlined at **4.4** above, modified to apply as follows:

(1) A designated HMRC officer must issue a notice of proposed counteraction to the responsible partner, stating that a return was made on the basis that a tax advantage arises to one or more partners from abusive tax arrangements and that it ought to be counteracted under the GAAR. A notice must:
- specify each of the partners in question (*'relevant partners'*), the arrangements and the tax advantage;
- explain why the officer considers that a tax advantage has arisen to each partner from the abusive arrangements;
- set out the counteraction that the officer considers ought to be taken;
- inform the responsible partner of the period for making representations (see (2) below); and
- explain the effect of the rules in (3)–(6) below and of the PENALTIES (**52.14**) which may apply if the proposed counteraction takes effect.

A notice may set out steps that could be taken to avoid the application of the GAAR.

If it subsequently appears to HMRC that the tax advantage has in fact not arisen to a particular partner, they must amend the notice accordingly and may take such other steps as they consider appropriate.

The adjustments specified in a notice have effect as if they were made under *FA 2013, s 209* (see **4.3** above under 'Effects of the GAAR'). This rule does not apply if a protective GAAR notice has already been given in respect of the specified adjustments (whether to the responsible partner as above or as in **4.5** above). The notice must normally be given within the normal time limits for assessments applicable to the proposed adjustments, but if the partnership return is under enquiry and the adjustments relate to matters included in the return, the notice can be given at any time until the time the enquiry is completed.

If no appeal is made in respect of the adjustments or an appeal is withdrawn or determined by agreement, and no final counteraction notice is given under (11) below or the provisions at **4.6** above, the notice has effect as if it were a final counteraction notice (and therefore, as if the procedural requirements had been met). A penalty under *FA*

2013, s 212B (see **52.14** PENALTIES) cannot, however, be charged. In any other case, the specified adjustments have no effect unless they (or lesser adjustments) are subsequently specified in a final counteraction notice. The time limits for making the final counteraction notice are treated as met by the giving of the original notice.

(2) The responsible partner has 45 days starting with the day on which HMRC's notice is given to send written representations in response to the notice to the designated HMRC officer. The designated officer may extend the period if the responsible partner makes a written request.

(3) Where the responsible partner amends the partnership return or a claim to counteract the tax advantage, and notifies HMRC accordingly, before the beginning of the closed period (see **4.3** above under 'Effect of the GAAR'), the matter is not referred to the GAAR Advisory Panel under (5) or (7) below. The responsible partner can amend a return or claim for this purpose during an enquiry even if the normal time limits have expired. No appeal may then be made against any enquiry closure notice (see **58.13** RETURNS) to the extent that it takes into account such an amendment. Where a responsible partner takes corrective action in this way, no penalty can be charged under the provisions at **52.14** PENALTIES.

(4) Where a relevant partner takes all necessary action to enter into a written agreement with HMRC to relinquish the tax advantage before the beginning of the closed period, that partner ceases to be treated as a relevant partner. HMRC must amend the original notice accordingly as soon as practicable after the closed period begins. If the partner then fails to enter into the written agreement, HMRC may proceed as if the partner continues to be a relevant partner (but without needing to amend the notice).

(5) If the responsible partner makes no representations, a designated HMRC officer must refer the matter to the GAAR Advisory Panel if the partner has not made the amendments in (3) above before the closed period begins and there remains at least one relevant partner.

The officer must at the same time notify the responsible partner that the matter is being referred. The notice must inform the responsible partner of the period for making representations under (8) below and of the requirement to send any such representations to the officer. The officer must provide the Panel with a copy of the notice given to the responsible partner at step (1) above and the notice informing the responsible partner that the matter has been referred to the Panel.

(6) If the responsible partner does make representations but has not made the amendments in (3) above before the closed period begins, then if there is at least one remaining relevant partner, the representations must be considered by a designated HMRC officer.

(7) If the designated HMRC officer in (6) above still considers that the GAAR should apply, he must refer the matter to the GAAR Advisory Panel, together with a copy of the responsible partner's representations and any comments he has on those representations. The officer must notify the responsible partner of his decision on whether or not to refer the matter to the GAAR Advisory Panel as soon as is reasonably practicable.

[4.7] Anti-Avoidance

The same requirements for the officer to notify the responsible partner and to provide information to the Panel apply as at step (5) above. The notice to the responsible partner must, however, also include a copy of any comments on the responsible partner's representations sent by the officer to the Panel.

(8) The responsible partner has 21 days to send written representations to the Panel and the designated HMRC officer about the notice given at step (1) above and any comments made by HMRC on the partner's original representations. The Panel may extend the period for making representations if the responsible partner makes a written request.

(9) If the responsible partner makes representations at step (8) above but did not make representations at step (2) above, the designated HMRC officer may provide the Panel and the responsible partner with comments on the step (8) representations.

(10) A sub-panel of three members of the Panel will consider the matter in question. The sub-panel may invite the responsible partner or the designated HMRC officer to supply further information within a specified period. Information supplied to the sub-panel must also be sent to the other party.

The sub-panel must produce an opinion notice stating its collective opinion as to whether or not the entering into and carrying out of the tax arrangements was a reasonable course of action in relation to the relevant tax provisions, having regard to the circumstances outlined at 4.3 above. An opinion notice may indicate that the sub-panel considers that it is not possible to reach a view on the information available. Alternatively, the sub-panel may produce two or three opinion notices which, taken together, state the opinions of all the members. An opinion notice must include the reasons for the opinion and is given to both the designated HMRC officer and the taxpayer.

(11) The designated HMRC officer must, having considered the sub-panel's opinion or opinions, give the responsible partner a written notice (a final counteraction notice) setting out whether or not the tax advantage under the arrangements is to be counteracted under the GAAR. It should be noted that HMRC are not bound by the decision of the sub-panel and may proceed with the application of the GAAR even if the sub-panel's opinion is that the GAAR ought not to apply.

If the GAAR is to apply, the final counteraction notice must specify the adjustments required and any steps that the responsible partner must take to give effect to them.

HMRC are not required to know for certain that a tax advantage has arisen before they embark on this procedure. They may carry out the above steps where a designated officer considers that a tax advantage might have arisen to a relevant partner. Any notice may be expressed to be given on the assumption that a tax advantage arises.

[FA 2013, ss 209ABA, 209AC, Sch 43, Sch 43D paras 5–9; FA 2021, Sch 32 paras 1, 4, 5].

Pooling notice or notice of binding given to responsible partner

If a designated HMRC officer considers that a partnership return has been made on the basis that a tax advantage has arisen to a partner (R) or to R and one or more other partners, and that officer has the power to give R a pooling notice or a notice of binding (see **4.6** above) in respect of the tax advantage, the notice may instead be given to the responsible partner. A pooling notice may not be given if a notice has been given under (1) above. A notice of binding may not be given if a pooling notice or a notice under (1) above has already been given.

The provisions at **4.6** above apply to a pooling notice or notice of binding given under the above provisions, with any necessary modifications.

In particular, a notice given under the above provisions must also specify the partners (the 'relevant partners') to which it applies. If it subsequently appears to HMRC that the tax advantage has in fact not arisen to a particular relevant partner, they must amend the notice accordingly and may take such other steps as they consider appropriate.

Where a responsible partner who has been given a pooling notice or a notice of binding amends the partnership return or a claim to counteract the tax advantage before the beginning of the 'closed period' (see **4.6** above), the partner is treated as not having been given the notice and the arrangements are accordingly no longer in the pool. A responsible partner can amend a return or claim for this purpose during an enquiry even if the normal time limits have expired. No appeal may then be made against any enquiry closure notice (see **58.13** RETURNS) to the extent that it takes into account such an amendment. The responsible partner must notify HMRC of the action taken.

Where a relevant partner takes all necessary action to enter into a written agreement with HMRC to relinquish the tax advantage before the beginning of the closed period, that partner ceases to be treated as a relevant partner. HMRC must amend the original notice accordingly as soon as practicable after the closed period begins. If the partner then fails to enter into the written agreement, HMRC may proceed as if the partner continues to be a relevant partner (but without needing to amend the notice).

Where, further to pooling notices given as above, two or more sets of arrangements are in a pool relating to any lead arrangements, and corrective action has been taken within the 75-day period beginning with the day on which the notice was given (or within such longer period as HMRC may have agreed) then, provided none of the pooled arrangements have been referred to the GAAR Advisory Panel individually, a designated HMRC officer may give to each of the taxpayers whose arrangements are in the pool a notice of a proposal to make a generic referral to the Panel in respect of the arrangements in the pool. The consequences of such a notice are the same as for a notice given under the provisions described under the heading 'Generic referral of equivalent arrangements to the GAAR Advisory Panel' at **4.6** above.

HMRC are not required to know for certain that a tax advantage has arisen before they give a notice, or do anything else, under these provisions. Any notice may be expressed to be given on the assumption that a tax advantage arises.

[FA 2013, Sch 43D paras 10–14; FA 2021, Sch 32 para 1].

[4.8] Anti-Avoidance

Specific legislation

[4.8] Specific anti-avoidance legislation is intended to counteract transactions designed to avoid tax, but genuine transactions may also sometimes be caught. The anti-avoidance provisions relating to capital gains tax and corporation tax on chargeable gains and described in this work are summarised in the table below and dealt with in detail in the paragraph indicated. Provisions which are targeted at a specific area of legislation or a relief are included in the relevant chapter; the remaining provisions are dealt with in this chapter.

Provision	Description	Para
Investment bond arrangements where the underlying asset is land. [*FA 2009, Sch 61 paras 20–22*].	Relief is not available where: (a) control of the underlying asset is acquired by a bond holder or a group of connected bond holders; or (b) the arrangements are not made for genuine commercial reasons or form part of arrangements for the avoidance of tax.	3.5 ALTERNATIVE FINANCE ARRANGEMENTS
Value shifting. [*TCGA 1992, s 29*].	A disposal of an asset is deemed to arise: (i) where a person exercises control of a company so that value passes out of shares or rights owned by him and passes into other shares or rights; (ii) where a property owner becomes the lessee of the property and there is a subsequent adjustment of the rights and liabilities under the lease favourable to the lessor; or (iii) on the abrogation or extinction of a right or restriction to which an asset is subject by the person entitled to enforce it. The consideration is the arm's length value received by the transferee.	4.9
Value shifting to give tax-free benefit. [*TCGA 1992, ss 30, 31*].	Applies to the disposal of an asset if a scheme or arrangements have been made whereby the asset's value has been materially reduced and a tax-free benefit arises to the person making the disposal, a connected person or, except where tax avoidance was not a main purpose, any other person. The consideration for the disposal is increased by a just and reasonable amount. Separate provisions apply to the disposal by a company of shares or securities of another company. See **4.12** below.	4.11, 4.12
Connected persons. [*TCGA 1992, s 18*].	A transaction between CONNECTED PERSONS (18) is treated as having been made by way of a non-arm's length bargain so that acquisition and disposal are treated as being made at market value in most cases. There are restrictions on losses in such circumstances.	4.13